THE POCKET BOOK OF
POEMS AND SONGS FOR THE OPEN AIR

EDWARD THOMAS

THE POCKET BOOK OF POEMS AND SONGS

FOR THE OPEN AIR

This edition first published in 2008
by Faber and Faber Ltd
3 Queen Square, London WC1N 3AU

This book is sold subject to the condition that it shall not, by way of
trade or otherwise, be lent, resold, hired out or otherwise circulated without
the publisher's prior consent in any form of binding or cover other than that in
which it is published and without a similar condition including this condition
being imposed on the subsequent purchaser

A CIP record for this book is available from the British Library

ISBN 978-0-571-24295-5

FOR HELEN

NOTE BY THE COMPILER

THIS Anthology is meant to please those lovers of poetry and the country who like a book that can always lighten some of their burdens or give wings to their delight, whether in the open air by day, or under the roof at evening ; for I have gathered into it much of the finest English poetry, and that poetry, at its best, can hardly avoid the open air. With this is some humbler poetry which is related to the finest as the grass to the stars : between the two I have often found it hard to choose. I have added about sixty of the sweetest songs which it seemed that a wise man would care to sing, or hear sung, in the fields, at the inn, on the road at dawn or nightfall, or at home. I need not defend the inclusion of some poems and songs that are not obviously connected with the country and some which are sorrowful. A lover has more ways of praising his mistress than by repeating the names of her virtues and lovely deeds ; and as to Sorrow —does she not often come to us as Joy blindfolded, and, in the end, withdraw her veil? The book, I hope, will endure the sunshine and the firelight, and give out an equal sweetness on the table and on the sward. I have chosen for my own pleasure, "whether wisely or no, let the forest judge."

The melodies are those which have come to please most my friends and myself, but I have not thought it necessary to include more than a few of such as are easily accessible and very well known. In only one or two cases have I admitted poor or corrupted words for the sake of a tune. For indispensable help in getting them at their sources I have to thank my friend Mr. A. Martin Freeman, who searched scores of Elizabethan and other song-books, and whose robust and delicate taste formed a standard which I have hardly ever ignored; and Mr. George Rathbone, who has helped me with the proofs and introduced me to several songs, including one or two which the admirable Westmorland festival has brought to light. These Westmorland songs have, I think, never been published before, except two of them in a book called "The Heart of England." "The Mowing Song," "The Whale," "Salt Beef," and "The Princess Royal" are also from an oral source. Some of the combinations of airs and words are Mr. Freeman's and mine, viz. "Meum est Propositum," "Marching Along," and "Three Men of Gotham."

I thank Miss Maud Aldis for the tune to "Rum and Milk"; Mr. H. Belloc for poems; the Rev. Jesse Berridge for the three new sea songs; Mr. Laurence Binyon for a poem from "The Death of

Adam" (Methuen & Co.); Messrs. Boosey and W. H. Gill for the air and words of "O what if the Fowler"; Mr. Gordon Bottomley for a poem from "The Gate of Smaragdus" (Elkin Mathews); Miss Lucy Broadwood and Mr. J. A. Fuller Maitland for a song from "English County Songs" (Leadenhall Press); Messrs. Chatto & Windus for two poems by O'Shaughnessy; Mr. Padraic Colum for a poem from "New Songs" (O'Donoghue, Dublin); Mr. Charles Dalmon for poems from his "Song Favours" and "Flower and Leaf"; Mr. John Davidson for a poem from "A Holiday and other Poems" (E. Grant Richards); Mr. William H. Davies for poems from his "Soul's Destroyer"; Mr. Bertram Dobell for a poem by Thomas Traherne; Mr. Gerald Gould for a poem from his "Lyrics" (David Nutt); Mr. Thomas Hardy for a poem from "Poems of the Past and Present" (Macmillan & Co.); Mrs. W. E. Henley for a poem from "Hawthorn and Lavender" (David Nutt); Mr. William Heinemann for a poem from Laurence Hope's "Indian Love"; Mr. Walter Hogg for a sonnet from "Meditata" (S. Welwood); Mr. A. E. Housman for a poem from "A Shropshire Lad" (E. Grant Richards); Mr. S. R. Lysaght for a poem from "Poems of the Unknown Way" (Macmillan & Co.); Messrs. Macmillan for poems by Christina Rossetti and T. E. Brown; Mr. Walter de la Mare for poems from "Songs of Childhood" (Longmans, Green & Co.) and

"Poems" (Murray); Mr. John Masefield for a poem from "Ballads" (Elkin Mathews) and one melody to "Spanish Ladies"; Mr. Elkin Mathews for a poem by Lionel Johnson; Mr. T. Sturge Moore for a poem from "The Little School"; the trustees of William Morris for a poem from "Songs by the Way" (Longmans, Green & Co.); Messrs. Methuen & Co. for a song from "A Garland of Country Song; Mr. Alfred Noyes for a poem from his "Poems" (Blackwood); Mr. Cecil Sharp and Rev. C. L. Marson for songs from their "Folk Songs from Somerset" (Simpkin, Marshall); and Mr. Sharp for one melody to "Spanish Ladies"; Mr. A. C. Swinburne for a poem from "Poems and Ballads" (Chatto & Windus); Mr. Arthur Symons for a poem from "The Fool of the World" (Heinemann); Mr. R. R. Terry for a sea song, "Let the Bulgine run"; Mr. Fisher Unwin for a poem by Amy Levy; Mr. W. B. Yeats for poems from "The Wind among the Reeds" (Elkin Mathews) and "Poems" (Fisher Unwin).

TABLE OF CONTENTS

THE INVITATION

		PAGE
REVEILLE	A. E. Housman	3
THE MERRY BEGGARS	Richard Brome	4
COME AWAY	Anonymous	5
MAKE HASTE, THEREFORE, SWEET LOVE	Edmund Spenser	6
WHITSUNTIDE	Anonymous	6
HUNTING SONG	Sir Walter Scott	7
THE DAISY	Geoffrey Chaucer	8
IN A LECTURE ROOM	Arthur Hugh Clough	10
CORINNA'S MAYING	Robert Herrick	10
EARLY RISING	William Barnes	13
LAUGHING SONG	William Blake	14
PER OMNIA DEUS	T. E. Brown	14
THE WRAGGLE TAGGLE GIPSIES, O!	Folk song	15
CORIDON'S SONG	Jo. Chalkhill	17
A-HUNTING WE WILL GO	Henry Fielding	19
THE HOLM BANK HUNTING SONG	Folk song	21
BLOW AWAY THE MORNING DEW	Folk song	23
JOG ON, JOG ON	William Shakespeare	25

THE START IN THE MORNING

		PAGE
A Country Muse	George Wither	29
The Child in the Story Awakes	Walter de la Mare	30
The Great Oak Tree that's in the Dell	William Barnes	31
The Day is Come	Percy Bysshe Shelley	33
Summer Dawn	William Morris	34
The Poet's Birth	Taliesin	35
The Retreat	Henry Vaughan	36
Wonder	Thomas Traherne	37
Keep Innocency	Walter de la Mare	39
Highway, My Parnassus	Sir P. Sidney	40
That's the Way	James Hogg	41
To the Morning	Richard Crashaw	42
Phœbus, Arise!	William Drummond	44
The Last Ride Together	Robert Browning	46
Spring Without Her	William Drummond	50
Fancy and Joy	Samuel Daniel	51
A Song of the Youths	Arthur O'Shaughnessy	51
The Merry Guide	A. E. Housman	53
Bunches of Grapes	Walter de la Mare	55
The Voice of the Mountain	Percy Bysshe Shelley	56
Inscription for a Fountain	Samuel Taylor Coleridge	61
Men are Fools that Wish to Die	Anonymous	62
Earth for its Own Sake	Lord Byron	62
Fancy's Birth	Shakespeare	64
Fancy	John Keats	65
July	Hilaire Belloc	68
To the Cuckoo	William Wordsworth	68
With Un-uplifted Eyes	William Wordsworth	70

		PAGE
THE PRINCE AND SPRING	Translated from *Howel ab Owain*	70
FROM "COMUS"	*John Milton*	71
THE NIGHTINGALE	*William Ernest Henley*	72
ROADWAYS	*John Masefield*	72
THE CHEERFUL HORN	*Folk song*	73
IN THE MERRY MONTH OF MAY	*Nicholas Breton*	75
EARLY ONE MORNING	*Anonymous*	76
LA FÊTE DES FOUS—LA PROSE DE L'ÂNE	*Anonymous*	77
DRUNKEN SAILOR	*Sea song*	79
MY COLLIER LADDIE	*Anonymous*	80
THE LINCOLNSHIRE POACHER	*Folk song*	81
THE WHALE	*Sea song*	83
LET THE BULLGINE RUN	*Sea song*	85
MOWING SONG	*Folk song*	86
RUM AND MILK	*Charles Dalmon*	87
MY LITTLE PRETTY ONE	*Anonymous*	88
MARCHING ALONG	*Robert Browning*	89

WAYSIDE REST

TO DIANEME	*Robert Herrick*	93
AN EXCELENTE BALADE OF CHARITIE	*Thomas Chatterton*	93
SONG	*Thomas Campion*	97
TO HIS COY MISTRESS	*Andrew Marvell*	98
WALY, WALY	*Anonymous*	99
FAREWELL TO ARMS	*George Peele*	101
SIR PATRICK SPENCE	*Anonymous*	102
SONG	*Anonymous*	103
PROTHALAMION	*Edmund Spenser*	104
ODE TO PSYCHE	*John Keats*	111

		PAGE
WILLY DROWNED IN YARROW	*Anonymous.*	113
SAE MERRY AS WE TWA HA'E BEEN	*Anonymous.*	115
UPON TWO GREENE APRICOCKES SENT TO COWLEY BY SIR CRASHAW	*Richard Crashaw*	116
MY LADY COMETH	*Geoffrey Chaucer.*	117
LA BELLE DAME SANS MERCI	*John Keats.*	118
YOUNG JOHN AND HIS TRUE SWEETHEART	*Anonymous*	120
A LOVE SONNET	*George Wither*	122
A NOBLE YOUTH	*Earl of Surrey*	124
THE PULLEY	*George Herbert*	126
ABSENT IN THE SPRING	*Shakespeare*	127
SONG	*Giles Fletcher*	128
THE BALLAD OF DOWSABELL	*Michael Drayton.*	129
THE LAMENT OF THE BORDER WIDOW	*Anonymous.*	134
ROSALIND MUSES	*Thomas Lodge*	135
SONG	*William Browne.*	136
SARRAZINE'S SONG OF PHARAMOND'S GRAVE	*Arthur O'Shaughnessy*	137
IN THE ORCHARD	*Algernon C. Swinburne*	139
O MISTRESS MINE	*William Shakespeare.*	141
LOVE WILL FIND OUT THE WAY	*Anonymous.*	142
SALLY IN OUR ALLEY	*H. Carey*	144
THE MESSAGE	*After John Donne*	147
THE SEAMEW	*From the Gaelic.*	148
BLOW, BLOW, THOU WINTER WIND	*William Shakespeare.*	148
ALL ROUND MY HAT	*Anonymous.*	149

		PAGE
O WHAT IF THE FOWLER	*Charles Dalmon* .	. 151
NOW, O NOW .	. *Anonymous* .	. 152
LIKE AS THE LARK	. *Anonymous* .	. 153
LA FILLE DU ROY .	. *Anonymous* .	. 154
AMARILLYS . .	. *Louis XIII, K. of France*	155
THE BAILIFF'S DAUGHTER OF ISLINGTON .	. *Anonymous* .	. 156
RIO GRANDE . .	. *Sea song* .	. 159

VILLAGE AND INN

CLARE'S DESIRE .	. *John Clare* .	. 163
FROM "THE GARDEN".	*Abraham Cowley* .	. 164
FROM "APPLETON HOUSE"	*Andrew Marvell*	. 165
THE WISH . .	. *Walter Pope* .	. 166
I GOT TWO FIELDS	. *William Barnes* .	. 168
FROM "THE CASTLE OF INDOLENCE" .	. *James Thomson* .	. 169
THE SUNFLOWER .	. *William Blake* .	. 172
TO PENSHURST .	. *Ben Jonson* .	. 172
EPITAPH: TEWKESBURY ABBEY . . .	. *Anonymous* .	. 176
UPON THE PRIORY GROVE, HIS USUAL RETIREMENT	*Henry Vaughan* .	. 176
A SAMPLER—LLANDDEUSAINT, CAERMARTHENSHIRE .		. 177
THE BELFRY . .	. *Laurence Binyon* .	. 178
CHURCH-MUSICK .	. *George Herbert* .	. 180
THE LITTLE VAGABOND .	*William Blake* .	. 181
EPITAPH ON AN INN-KEEPER . .	. *Anonymous* .	. 182
A TAVERN RHYME .	. *Anonymous* .	. 182
EPITAPH IN A CORNISH CHURCHYARD .	. *Anonymous* .	. 183

		PAGE
LUBBER BREEZE	*T. Sturge Moore*	183
MARIANA	*Lord Tennyson*	184
A NEW YEAR CAROL	*Anonymous*	187
THE FAIRIES' FAREWELL	*Richard Corbet*	187
DRINKING SONGS	*John Still, Bishop of Bath and Wells*	190
	Anonymous	191
WRITTEN AT AN INN AT HENLEY	*William Shenstone*	192
THE VILLAGE SHOP	*William Shenstone*	193
THE HOCK-CART, OR HARVEST HOME	*Robert Herrick*	194
THREE DRINKING SONGS	*John Marston*	196
	William H. Davies	197
	Hilaire Belloc	198
THE MILKMAID	*Thomas Nabbes*	199
MERRY MARGARET	*John Skelton*	199
THE VILLAGE SCHOOLMISTRESS	*William Shenstone*	201
THE SOLITARY REAPER	*William Wordsworth*	202
FROM "THE STEELE GLASSE"	*George Gascoigne*	203
THE LEECH GATHERER	*William Wordsworth*	204
ANIMALS	*Walt Whitman*	209
THE WHITE ISLAND	*Robert Herrick*	210
WELCOME	*John Fletcher*	211
COME, SWEET LASS	*Anonymous*	212
SLEDBURN FAIR	*Folk song*	213
DICKY OF TAUNTON DEAN	*Folk song*	214
JACK AND JOAN	*Thomas Campion*	217
WHO LIVETH SO MERRY	*Anonymous*	218
POOR OLD HORSE	*Folk song*	220
THE JOLLY WAGGONER	*Folk song*	222
THE HAYMAKERS' CHORUS	*Folk song*	222
MEUM EST PROPOSITUM	*Anonymous*	223

		PAGE
SALT BEEF . . . *Sea song* . .	. 224
THE "PRINCESS ROYAL" *Sea song* .	. 225
SOLDIERS THREE . . *Anonymous* . .	. 227

THE FOOTPATH

TO VIOLETS . . . *Robert Herrick* .	. 231
SWEET BIRD . . . *William Drummond*	. 231
THE PLOUGHER . . *Padraic Colum* .	. 232
A FAERY SONG . . *W. B. Yeats* .	. 233
LINES FROM THE "MILTON" OF WILLIAM BLAKE	234
THE BIRCH-TREE AT LOSCHWITZ . . *Amy Levy* . .	. 235
ATAVISM . . . *Laurence Hope* ("Indian Love": Heinemann).	236
CA' THE YOWES TO THE KNOWES . . . *Isobel Pagan* .	. 236
THE HARBOUR . . *William Browne* .	. 238
O'ER THE MOOR AMANG THE HEATHER . . *Jean Glover* .	. 238
REMEMBERED SPRING . From the Welsh of Llywarch Hên	. 240
THE LADY OF SHALOTT *Alfred, Lord Tennyson*	240
CORNISH WIND . . *Arthur Symons* .	. 247
LINES FROM THE "MILTON" OF WILLIAM BLAKE	248
LINES FROM "THE SOUL'S DESTROYER" . . *William H. Davies*	. 249
SONGS FROM "THE HOLLOW LAND" . . *William Morris* .	. 250
FROM "EPIPSYCHIDION" *Percy Bysshe Shelley*	. 251
MALVOLIO . . . *Walter Savage Landor*	. 254
DAFFADILL . . . *Michael Drayton* .	. 255
THE DREAM GARDEN . *Geoffrey Chaucer* .	. 256
LINES TO A DRAGON-FLY *Walter Savage Landor*	257
TO JOHN POINS . . *Sir Thomas Wyatt*	. 258

		PAGE
TO THE CUCKOO	*John Logan*	259
THE QUESTION	*Percy Bysshe Shelley*	260
TO THE RIVER DUDDON:		
FAREWELL	*William Wordsworth*	262
YEW TREES	*William Wordsworth*	263
A SEA CHANGE	*Walter Hogg*	264
NUTTING	*William Wordsworth*	264
UNDER THE LIME TREE	*Thomas Lovell Beddoes*	266
POPULOUS SOLITUDE	*Hartley Coleridge*	268
A SOLITUDE WITHIN A SOLITUDE	*Christina Rossetti*	268
TWEED AND TILL	*Anonymous*	269
A RUNNABLE STAG	*John Davidson*	269
THE DAIRYMAIDS TO PAN	*Gordon Bottomley*	273
THE BIRTH OF ROBIN HOOD	*Anonymous*	274
THE BOLD PEDLAR AND ROBIN HOOD	*Anonymous*	277
ROBIN HOOD'S FUNERAL	*Anthony Munday*	279
FULL SUMMER	*George Peele*	280
MEG MERRILIES	*John Keats*	280
UN ROSEAU PENSANT	*John Lyly*	281
SIR LANCELOT AND QUEEN GUINEVERE	*Lord Tennyson*	282
THE MOODS	*W. B. Yeats*	284
SONG	*Francis Beaumont*	284
THE ANGLER'S SONG	*Izaak Walton*	284
AS I WALKED FORTH	*Anonymous*	285
DABBLING IN THE DEW	*Folk song*	287
SWEET PRIMEROSES	*Folk song*	288
A-BEGGING WE WILL GO	*Anonymous*	290
GREENSLEEVES	*Anonymous*	291
LOVE'S THRALDOM	*Anonymous*	294
TOBACCO IS AN INDIAN WEED	*Anonymous*	295

EVENING

		PAGE
VESPERS	*T. E. Brown*	299
BAGLEY WOOD	*Lionel Johnson*	299
WITH HOW SAD STEPS, O MOON	*Sir Philip Sidney*	300
SONG	*Alfred Noyes*	301
AUTUMN	*William H. Davies*	301
TO THE MOON	*Percy Bysshe Shelley*	302
A SUMMER'S EVE	*Henry Kirke White*	303
LULLABY	*George Gascoigne*	305
TRANQUILLITY	*William Shakespeare*	306
TO NIGHT	*Percy Bysshe Shelley*	307
KUBLA KHAN	*Samuel Taylor Coleridge*	308
TO AUTUMN	*John Keats*	310
AUTUMN	*William Blake*	311
AVE MARIA!	*Lord Byron*	312
MILKING TIME	*Charles Dalmon*	315
ROMANCE	*Gerald Gould*	316
THE POET IN THE CLOUDS	*Samuel Taylor Coleridge*	316
THE UNEXPLORED	*Sidney Royse Lysaght*	317
THE DARKLING THRUSH	*Thomas Hardy*	319
VERTUE	*George Herbert*	321
THIS ONLY GRANT ME	*Abraham Cowley*	321
THE MESSAGE OF THE MARCH WIND	*William Morris*	322
HARVEST HOME	*Folk song*	326
SPANISH LADIES	*Sea song*	327
MALT	*Anonymous*	329
WHEN THE KING ENJOYS HIS OWN AGAIN	*Martin Parker*	330
WHEN THOU MUST HOME	*Thomas Campion*	332
THREE MEN OF GOTHAM	*Thomas Love Peacock*	333
SUMMER IS ICUMEN IN	*Anonymous*	334

THE INVITATION

Reveille

WAKE: the silver dusk returning
   Up the beach of darkness brims,
And the ship of sunrise burning
   Strands upon the eastern rims.

Wake: the vaulted shadow shatters,
   Trampled to the floor it spanned,
And the tent of night in tatters
   Straws the sky-pavilioned land.

Up, lad, up, 'tis late for lying:
   Hear the drums of morning play;
Hark, the empty highways crying
   "Who'll beyond the hills away?"

Towns and countries woo together,
   Forelands beacon, belfries call;
Never lad that trod on leather
   Lived to feast his heart with all.

Up, lad: thews that lie and cumber
   Sunlit pallets never thrive;
Morns abed and daylight slumber
   Were not meant for man alive.

Clay lies still, but blood's a rover:
   Breath's a ware that will not keep.
Up, lad: when the journey's over
   There'll be time enough for sleep.

A. E. Housman.

The Merry Beggars

COME, come away! the spring,
  By every bird that can but sing
Or chirp a note, doth now invite
Us forth to taste of his delight,
In field, in grove, on hill, in dale;
But above all the nightingale,
Who in her sweetness strives t' outdo
The loudness of the hoarse cuckoo.
  "Cuckoo," cries he; "Jug, jug," sings she;
    From bush to bush, from tree to tree:
    Why in one place then tarry we?

Come away! why do we stay?
We have no debt or rent to pay;
No bargains or accounts to make,
Nor land or lease to let or take:
Or if we had, should that remore us
When all the world's our own before us,
And where we pass and make resort,
It is our kingdom and our court?
  "Cuckoo," cries he; "Jug, jug," sings she;
    From bush to bush, from tree to tree:
    Why in one place then tarry we?

Richard Brome.

Come Away

COME away, come sweet Love,
  The golden morning breakes:
All the earth, all the ayre
Of love and pleasure speakes.
Teach thine arms then to embrace,
And sweet rosie lips to kisse:
And mix our soules in mutual blisse.
Eyes were made for beautie's grace,
Viewing, ruing love's long paine:
Procur'd by beautie's rude disdaine.

Come away, come sweet Love,
The golden morning wasts:
While the sunne from his sphere
His fierie arrowes casts,
Making all the shadowes flie,
Playing, staying in the grove,
To entertaine the stealth of love—
Thither, sweet love, let us hie
Flying, dying in desire,
Wing'd with sweet hopes and heavenly fire.

Come away, come sweet Love,
Doe not in vain adjorne
Beautie's grace that should rise,
Like to the naked morne.
Lillies on the river's side,
And faire Cyprian flowers newe blowne
Desire no beauties but their owne.
Ornament is nurse of pride.
Pleasure, measure, Love's delight:
Haste, then, sweet Love, our wished flight.

Anonymous.

Make haste, therefore, sweet Love

FRESH Spring, the herald of loves mighty king,
  In whose cote-armour richly are displayd
All sorts of flowers, the which on earth do spring,
  In goodly colours gloriously arrayd—
Goe to my love, where she is carelesse layd,
Yet in her winters bowre not well awake ;
Tell her the joyous time wil not be staid,
Unlesse she doe him by the forelock take ;
Bid her therefore her selfe soone ready make
To wayt on Love amongst his lovely crew ;
Where every one, that misseth then her make,
Shall be by him amearst with penance dew.
  Make hast, therefore, sweet love, whilest it is prime,
  For none can call againe the passèd time.

Edmund Spenser.

Whitsuntide

IN somer when the shawes be sheyne,
  And leves be large and long,
Hit is full merry in feyre foreste
  To here the foulys song.

To se the dere draw to the dale
  And leve the hilles hee,
And shadow him in the leves grene
  Under the green-wode tree.

Hit befell on Whitson tide
    Early in a May mornyng,
The Sonne up faire can shyne,
    And the briddis mery can syng.

"This is a mery mornyng," said Litulle Johne,
    "Be Hym that dyed on tre;
A more mery man than I am one
    Lyves not in Christiantè.

"Pluk up thi hert, my dere mayster,"
    Litulle Johne can say,
"And thynk hit is a fulle fayre tyme
    In a mornynge of May."
Anonymous.

Hunting Song

WAKEN, lords and ladies gay,
    On the mountain dawns the day;
All the jolly chase is here
With hawk and horse and hunting-spear;
Hounds are in the couples yelling,
Hawks are whistling, horns are knelling,
Merrily, merrily mingle they,
    "Waken, lords and ladies gay."

Waken, lords and ladies gay,
The mist has left the mountains gray,
Springlets in the dawn are steaming,
Diamonds on the brake are gleaming,

And foresters have busy been
To track the buck in thicket green;
Now we come to chant our lay,
    "Waken, lords and ladies gay."

Waken, lords and ladies gay,
To the greenwood haste away;
We can show you where he lies,
Fleet of foot and tall of size;
We can show the marks he made
When 'gainst the oak his antlers fray'd;
You shall see him brought to bay;
    Waken, lords and ladies gay.

Louder, louder chant the lay
Waken, lords and ladies gay!
Tell them youth and mirth and glee
Run a course as well as we;
Time, stern huntsman! who can baulk,
Stanch as hound and fleet as hawk;
Think of this, and rise with day,
    Gentle lords and ladies gay!
                              Sir Walter Scott.

The Daisy ～ ～ ～ ～

AND as for me, though that I konne but lyte,
    On bokés for to rede I me delyte,
And to hem yive I feyth and ful credence,
And in myn herte have hem in reverence

So hertély, that there is gamé noon
That fro my bokés maketh me to goon,
But it be seldom on the holy day,
Save, certeynly, whan that the month of May
Is comen, and that I here the foulés synge
And that the flourés gynnen for to sprynge,—
Farewel my boke, and my devocion!

Now have I thanne suche a condicion,
That of alle the flourés in the mede,
Than love I most thise flourés white and rede,
Such as men callen daysyes in our toun.
To hem have I so grete affeccioun,
As I seyde erst, whan comen is the May,
That in my bed ther daweth me no day,
That I nam up and walkyng in the mede,
To seen this floure agein the sonné sprede,
When it uprysith erly by the morwe;
That blisful sighté softneth all my sorwe,
So glad am I, whan that I have presence
Of it, to doon it allé reverence,
As she that is of allé flourés floure,
Fulfilléd of al vertue and honour,
And evere iliké faire, and fresshe of hewe.
And I love it, and evere yliké newe,
And ever shal, til that myn herté dye;
Al swere I nat, of this I wol nat lye;
Ther lovéd no wight hotter in his lyve.

And when that it is eve, I renné blyve,
As soon as evere the sonné gynneth weste,
To seen this flour, how it wol go to reste,
For fere of nyght, so hateth she derknesse!

Hir chere is pleynly sprad in the brightnesse
Of the sonné, for ther it wol unclose.
Allas, that I ne had Englyssh, ryme or prose,
Suffisant this flour to preyse aryght!

Geoffrey Chaucer.

In a Lecture Room

AWAY, haunt thou not me,
   Thou vain Philosophy!
Little hast thou bestead,
Save to perplex the head,
And leave the spirit dead.
Unto thy broken cisterns wherefore go,
While from the secret treasure-depths below,
Fed by the skiey shower,
And clouds that sink and rest on hill-tops high,
Wisdom at once, and Power,
Are welling, bubbling forth, unseen, incessantly?
Why labour at the dull mechanic oar,
When the fresh breeze is blowing,
And the strong current flowing,
Right onward to the Eternal Shore?

Arthur Hugh Clough.

Corinna's Maying

GET up, get up for shame! The blooming morn
   Upon her wings presents the god unshorn.
  See how Aurora throws her fair
  Fresh-quilted colours through the air:

    Get up, sweet Slug-a-bed, and see
    The dew bespangling herb and tree.
Each flower has wept, and bow'd toward the east,
Above an hour since ; yet you not drest,
    Nay ! not so much as out of bed ?
    When all the birds have matins said,
    And sung their thankful hymns : 'tis sin,
    Nay, profanation, to keep in,—
Whenas a thousand virgins on this day,
Spring, sooner than the lark, to fetch in May.

Rise ; and put on your foliage, and be seen
To come forth, like the Spring-time, fresh and green,
    And sweet as Flora. Take no care
    For jewels for your gown, or hair :
    Fear not ; the leaves will strew
    Gems in abundance upon you :
Besides, the childhood of the day has kept,
Against you come, some orient pearls unwept :
    Come, and receive them while the light
    Hangs on the dew-locks of the night :
    And Titan on the eastern hill
    Retires himself, or else stands still
Till you come forth. Wash, dress, be brief in praying :
Few beads are best, when once we go a Maying.

Come, my Corinna, come ; and coming, mark
How each field turns a street ; each street a park
    Made green, and trimm'd with trees : see how
    Devotion gives each house a bough

    Or branch : each porch, each door, ere this,
      An ark, a tabernacle is,
Made up of white-thorn neatly interwove ;
As if here were those cooler shades of love.
    Can such delights be in the street,
    And open fields, and we not see't?
    Come, we'll abroad ; and let's obey
    The proclamation made for May :
And sin no more, as we have done, by staying ;
But, my Corinna, come, let's go a Maying.

There's not a budding boy, or girl, this day,
But is got up, and gone to bring in May.
    A deal of youth, ere this, is come
    Back, and with white-thorn laden home.
    Some have dispatch'd their cakes and cream,
    Before that we have left to dream :
And some have wept, and woo'd, and plighted troth,
And chose their priest, ere we can cast off sloth :
    Many a green-gown has been given ;
    Many a kiss, both odd and even :
    Many a glance, too, has been sent
    From out the eye, love's firmament :
Many a jest told of the keys betraying
This night, and locks pick'd :—Yet we're not a
    Maying.

Come, let us go, while we are in our prime ;
And take the harmless folly of the time !
    We shall grow old apace, and die
    Before we know our liberty.

Our life is short ; and our days run
 As fast away as does the sun :—
And as a vapour, or a drop of rain
Once lost, can ne'er be found again :
 So when or you or I are made
 A fable, song, or fleeting shade ;
 All love, all liking, all delight
 Lies drown'd with us in endless night.
Then while time serves, and we are but decaying,
Come, my Corinna ! come, let's go a Maying.
Robert Herrick.

Early Rising

THE aïr to gi'e your cheäks a hue
 O' rwosy red, so feaïr to view,
Is what do sheäke the grass-bleädes grae
At breäk o' dae, in mornén dew ;
Vor vo'k that will be rathe abrode,
Will meet wi' health upon their road.

But biden up till dead o' night,
When han's o' clocks do stan' upright,
By candlelight, do soon consume
The feäce's bloom, an' turn it white.
An' moon-beäms cast vrom midnight skies
Do blunt the sparklen ov the eyes.

Vor health do weäke vrom nightly dreams
Below the mornen's eärly beams,

An' leäve the dead-aïr'd houses' eaves,
Vor quiv'ren leaves, an' bubblen streams,
A-glitt'ren brightly to the view,
Below a sky o' cloudless blue.

William Barnes.

Laughing Song

WHEN the green woods laugh with the voice of joy,
And the dimpling stream runs laughing by ;
When the air does laugh with our merry wit,
And the green hill laughs with the noise of it ;

When the meadows laugh with lively green,
And the grasshopper laughs in the merry scene ;
When Mary and Susan and Emily
With their sweet round mouths sing " Ha ha he ! "

When the painted birds laugh in the shade,
Where our table with cherries and nuts is spread :
Come live, and be merry, and join with me,
To sing the sweet chorus of " Ha ha he ! "

William Blake.

Per Omnia Deus

WHAT moves at Cardiff, how a man
At Newport ends the day as he began,
At Weston what adventure may befall,
What Bristol dreams, or if she dream at all,

Upon the pier, with step sedate,
I meditate—
Poor souls! whose God is Mammon—
Meanwhile, from Ocean's gate,
Keen for the foaming spate,
The true God rushes in the Salmon.

T. E. Brown.

The Wraggle Taggle Gipsies, O!

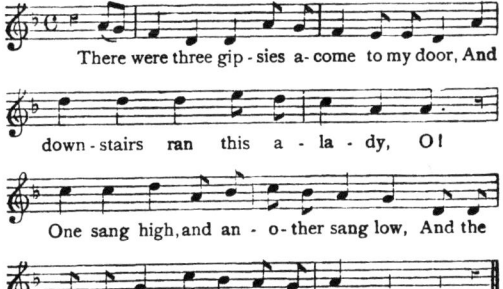

From "Folk Songs from Somerset." Gathered and edited by Cecil J. Sharp and Charles L. Marson

There were three gip-sies a-come to my door, And down-stairs ran this a-la-dy, O! One sang high, and an-o-ther sang low, And the o-ther sang bon-ny, bon-ny Bis-cay, O!

II

Then she pulled off her silk-finished gown
And put on hose of leather, O!
The ragged, ragged rags about our door—
She's gone with the wraggle taggle gipsies, O!

III

It was late last night, when my lord came home,
Enquiring for his a-lady, O !
The servants said, on every hand :
She's gone with the wraggle taggle gipsies, O !

IV

O saddle to me my milk-white steed.
Go and fetch me my pony, O !
That I may ride and seek my bride,
Who is gone with the wraggle taggle gipsies, O !

V

O he rode high and he rode low,
He rode through woods and copses too,
Until he came to an open field,
And there he espied his a-lady, O !

VI

What makes you leave your house and land?
What makes you leave your money, O ?
What makes you leave your new-wedded lord ;
To go with the wraggle taggle gipsies, O ?

VII

What care I for my house and my land?
What care I for my money, O ?
What care I for my new-wedded lord ?
I'm off with the wraggle taggle gipsies, O !

VIII

Last night you slept on a goose-feather bed,
With the sheet turned down so bravely, O !
And to-night you'll sleep in a cold open field,
Along with the wraggle taggle gipsies, O !

IX

What care I for a goose-feather bed,
With the sheet turned down so bravely, O?
For to-night I shall sleep in a cold open field,
Along with the wraggle taggle gipsies, O!

Coridon's Song

Oh, the sweet content-ment the country-man doth find! Heigh trol-lol-lie lol-lie loe, Heigh trol-lol-lie loe! It's qui-et con-tem-pla-tion possesseth all my mind: Then Care away, Care away, Care a-way, And wend a-long with me.

II

For Courts are full of Flatt'ry,
As hath too oft been try'd,
    Heigh, etc.
Of Wantonness the City,
And both are full of Pride.
    Then Care away, etc.

III

But Oh! the honest Peasant
Speaks truly from his Heart,
    Heigh, etc.
His Pride is in his Tillage,
His Horses, Plough and Cart.
    Then Care away, etc.

IV

Our Dress is good plain Sheepskins,
Grey Russet for our wives.
    Heigh, etc.
'Tis Warmth, and not gay Cloathing,
Prolongs our Strength and Lives.
    Then Care away, etc.

V

The Clown, though hard he labour,
Yet on the Holiday—
    Heigh, etc.
No Emperor so merrily
Can pass his time away.
    Then Care away, etc.

VI

To recompense our Tillage
The Heav'ns afford us show'rs;
    Heigh, etc.
And for our sweet Refreshments
The Earth gives verdant Bow'rs
    Then Care away, etc.

VII

The Cuckow, Lark and Nightingale
In merry Concerts sing,
    Heigh, etc.
And with their pleasant Roundelays
Give welcome to the Spring.
    Then Care away, etc.

VIII

This is not Half the Happiness
We jovial Rustics see ;
    Heigh, etc.
If others think they have as much
He lies—whoe'er he be :
    Then come away, come away, come away,
        Turn Countryman with me.

Jo. Chalkhill.

Altered and set to music by Moses Browne, 1772.

A-Hunting we will go

The dusky night rides down the sky, And ush-ers in the morn; The hounds all join in glo-rious cry, The hounds all join in glorious cry, The huntsman blows his

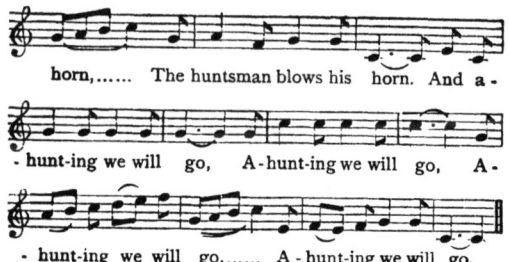

horn,...... The huntsman blows his horn. And a-hunt-ing we will go, A-hunt-ing we will go, A-hunt-ing we will go,...... A-hunt-ing we will go.

II

The wife around her husband throws
   Her arms and begs his stay:
My dear, it rains, it hails, it snows,
   You will not hunt to-day?
      But a-hunting we will go.

III

A brushing fox in yonder wood
   Secure to find we seek,
For why, I carried sound and good
   A cartload there last week.
      And a-hunting we will go.

IV

Away he goes, he flies the rout,
   Their steeds all spur and switch,
Some are thrown in and some thrown out,
   And some thrown in the ditch.
      But a-hunting we will go.

V

At length, his strength to faintness worn,
  Poor Reynard ceases flight,
Then, hungry, homeward we return
  To feast away the night.
     Then a-drinking we do go.

Henry Fielding.

The Holm Bank Hunting Song

Westmorland

One morning last winter to Holm-bank there came A brave noble sportsman, Squire Sands was his name, Came hunt-ing the fox, bold Reynard must die, And he flung out his train and began for to cry, Tally ho! tal-ly ho! ...... Hark, for-ward a-way, tal-ly ho!

II

The season being frosty, and the morning being clear,
A great many gentlemen appoint to meet there;
To meet with Squire Sandys with honour and fame
And his dogs in their glory to honour his name.

III

There Gaby the huntsman with his horn in his hand,
It sounded so clear and the dogs at command,
Tantivy, tantivy! the horn it did sound,
Which alarmed the country for above a mile round.

IV

It's hark dogs together, while Juno comes in;
There's Joyful and Frolic, likewise little Trim,
It's hark unto Dinah, the bitch that runs fleet;
There's neat little Justice, she'll set 'em to reet

V

There's Driver and Gamester, two excellent hounds,
They'll find out bold Reynard if he lies above ground;
Draw down to yonder cover that lies to the south;
Bold Reynard lies there! Trowler doubles his mouth.

VI

Three times round Low Furness they chased him full hard;
At last he sneaked off and through Urswick churchyard;
He listened to the singers (as I've heard them say),
But the rest of the service he could not well stay. . . .

VII

Through Kirkby and Woodland they nimbly passed;
Broughton and Dunnerdale they came to at last;
Then down across Duddon to Cumberland side,
And at Grassgards in Ulpha bold Reynard he died.

VIII

Since Reynard is dead he will do no more ill;
He hadn't much time for to make a long will;
He has left all his states to his survivor and heir,
He has a right to a widow, for she'll claim her share.

IX

Of such a fox chase there never was known,—
The horsemen and footmen were instantly thrown;
To keep within sound didn't lie in their power,
For the dogs chased the fox eighty miles in five hours.

X

You gentlemen and sportsmen, wherever you be,
All you that love hunting, draw near unto me,
Since Reynard is dead, we have heard his downfall,
Here's a health to Squire Sandys of High Grathwaite Hall.

>Tally ho, tally ho! Hark forward, away, tally ho!

Blow away the Morning Dew

From "Folk Songs from Somerset." Gathered and edited by Cecil J. Sharp and Charles L. Marson

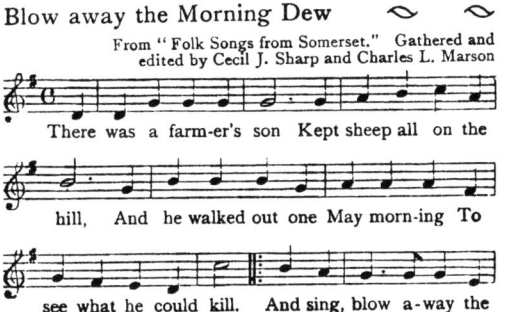

There was a farm-er's son Kept sheep all on the hill, And he walked out one May morn-ing To see what he could kill. And sing, blow a-way the

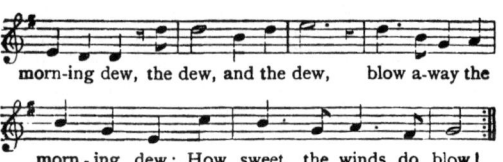

morn-ing dew, the dew, and the dew, blow a-way the morn-ing dew; How sweet the winds do blow!

II

He lookèd high he lookèd low,
He cast an under look;
And there he saw a fair pretty maid
Beside the watery brook.
    And sing, etc.

III

Cast over me my mantle fair
And pin it o'er my gown;
And, if you will, take hold my hand
And I will be your own.
    And sing, etc.

IV

If you come down to my father's house,
Which is wallèd all around,
There you shall have a kiss from me
And twenty thousand pound.
    And sing, etc.

V

He mounted on a milk-white steed
And she upon another,
And then they rode along the lane
Like sister and like brother.
    And sing, etc.

VI

As they were riding all alone
They saw some pooks of hay,
O is not this a very pretty place
For the boys and girls to play?
  And sing, etc.

VII

But when they came to her father's gate,
So nimble she popped in,
And said : There is a fool without
And here's the maid within.
  And sing, etc.

VIII

We have a flower in our gardèn,
We call it Marygold ;
And if you will not when you may,
You shall not when you wolde.
  And sing, etc.

Jog on, Jog on

Jog on, jog on the foot-path way, And
mer-ri-ly hent the stile-a! Your mer-ry heart goes
all the day, And your sad heart tires in a mile-a!

II

Your paltry money-bags of gold
What need have we to stare for?
When little or nothing soon is told,
And we have the less to care for.

III

Cast care away, let sorrow cease,
A fig for melancholy;
Let's laugh and sing, or, if you please,
We'll frolic with sweet Dolly.

THE START IN THE MORNING

A Country Muse

IN my former days of bliss,
  Her divine skill taught me this:
That from everything I saw
I could some invention draw,
And raise pleasure to the height,
Through the meanest object's sight.
By the murmur of a spring,
Or the least bough's rusteling;
By a daisy whose leaves spread
Shut when Titan goes to bed,
Or a shady bush or tree,
She could more infuse in me
Than all Nature's beauties can
In some other wiser man. . . .
Poesy, thou sweet'st content
That e'er heav'n to mortals lent,
Though they as a trifle leave thee
Whose dull thoughts cannot conceive thee,
Though thou be to them a scorn
That to nought but earth are born,
Let my life no longer be
Than I am in love with thee.

George Wither.

The Child in the Story Awakes

THE light of dawn rose on my dreams,
    And from afar I seemed to hear
In sleep the mellow blackbird call
    Hollow and sweet and clear.

I prythee, Nurse, my casement open,
    Wildly the garden peals with singing,
And hooting through the dewy pines
    The goblins all are winging.

O listen the droning of the bees,
    That in the roses take delight!
And see a cloud stays in the blue
    Like an angel still and bright.

The gentle sky is spread like silk,
    And, Nurse, the moon doth languish there,
As if it were a perfect jewel
    In the morning's soft-spun hair.

The greyness of the distant hills
    Is silvered in the lucid East,
See, now the sheeny-plumèd cock
    Wags haughtily his crest.

"O come you out, O come you out,
    Lily, and lavender, and lime;
The kingcup swings his golden bell,
    And plumpy cherries drum the time.

"O come you out, O come you out!
    Roses, and dew, and mignonette,
The sun is in the steep blue sky,
    Sweetly the morning star is set."

Walter de la Mare.

The Great Oak Tree that's in the Dell

THE girt woak tree that's in the dell !
   There's noo tree I do love so well ;
Vor times an' times when I wer young,
I there've a-climbed, an' there've a-zwung,
An' pick'd the eäcorns green, a-shed
In wrestlèn storms vrom his broad head.
An' down below's the cloty brook
Where I did vish with line and hook,
An' beät, in playsome dips and zwims,
The foamy stream, wi' white-skinn'd lim's.
An' there my mother nimbly shot
Her knitten-needles as she zot
At evenèn doun below the wide
Woak's head, wi' father at her zide.
An' I've a played wi' many a bwoy,
That's now a man an' gone awoy ;
    Zoo I do like noo tree so well
    'S the girt woak tree that's in the dell.

An' there, in leäter years, I roved
Wi' thik poor maïd I fondly loved,—
The maïd too feäir to die so soon,—
When evenèn twilight, or the moon,
Cast light enough 'ithin the pleäce
To show the smiles upon her feäce,
Wi' eyes so clear's the glassy pool,
An' lips an' cheäks so soft as wool.
There han' in han', wi bosoms warm,
Wi' love that burn'd but thought noo harm.

Below the wide-bough'd tree we past
The happy hours that went too vast;
An' though she'll never be my wife,
She's still my leäden star o' life.
She's gone: an' she've a-left to me
Her mem'ry in the girt woak tree;
    Zoo I do love noo tree so well
      'S the girt woak tree that's in the dell.

An' oh! mid never ax nor hook
Be brought to spweil his steätely look;
Nor ever roun' his ribby zides
Mid cattle rub ther heäiry hides;
Nor pigs rout up his turf, but keep
His lwonesome sheäde vor harmless sheep;
An' let en grow, an' let en spread,
An' let en live when I be dead.
But oh! if men should come an' vell
The girt woak tree that's in the dell,
An' build his planks 'ithin the zide
O' zome girt ship to plough the tide,
Then, life or death! I'd goo to sea,
A sailèn wi' the girt woak tree:
An' I upon his planks would stand,
An' die a-fightèn vor the land,—
The land so dear,—the land so free—
The land that bore the girt woak tree;
    Vor I do love noo tree so well
      'S the girt woak tree that's in the dell.

William Barnes.

From "Epipsychidion"

THE day is come, and thou wilt fly with me,
  To whatsoe'er of dull mortality
Is mine, remain a vestal sister still;
To the intense, the deep, the imperishable,
Not mine but me, henceforth be thou united
Even as a bride, delighting and delighted.
The hour is come:—the destined star is risen
Which shall descend upon a vacant prison.
The walls are high, the gates are strong, thick set
The sentinels—but true love never yet
Was thus constrained: it overleaps all fence:
Like lightning, with invisible violence
Piercing its continents; like Heaven's free breath,
Which he who grasps can hold not; liker Death,
Who rides upon a thought, and makes his way
Through temple, tower, and palace, and the array
Of arms: more strength has Love than he or they;
For it can burst his charnel, and make free
The limb in chains, the heart in agony,
The soul in dust and chaos.
                              Emily,
A ship is floating in the harbour now,
A wind is hovering o'er the mountain's brow;
There is a path on the sea's azure floor,
No keel has ever ploughed that path before;
The halcyons brood around the foamless isles;
The treacherous Ocean has forsworn its wiles;
The merry mariners are bold and free:
Say, my heart's sister, wilt thou sail with me?

Our bark is as an albatross, whose nest
Is a far Eden of the purple East;
And we between her wings will sit, while Night
And Day, and Storm and Calm, pursue their flight
Our ministers, along the boundless sea,
Treading each other's heels, unheededly.

Percy Bysshe Shelley.

Summer Dawn ᵕ ᵕ ᵕ

PRAY but one prayer for me 'twixt thy closed lips,
 Think but one thought of me up in the stars.
The summer night waneth, the morning light slips,
 Faint and grey 'twixt the leaves of the aspen, betwixt the cloud-bars,
That are patiently waiting there for the dawn:
 Patient and colourless, though Heaven's gold
Waits to float through them along with the sun.
Far out in the meadows, above the young corn,
 The heavy elms wait, and restless and cold
The uneasy wind rises; the roses are dun;
Through the long twilight they pray for the dawn,
Round the lone house in the midst of the corn.
 Speak but one word to me over the corn,
 Over the tender, bow'd locks of the corn.

William Morris.

The Poet's Birth

PRIMARY chief bard am I to Elphin,
   And my original country is the region of the summer stars;
Idno and Heinin called me Merddin,
At length every king will call me Taliesin.
I was with my Lord in the highest sphere,
On the fall of Lucifer into the depth of hell;
I have borne a banner before Alexander;
I know the names of the stars from north to south;
I have been on the galaxy at the throne of the Distributor . . .
I have been with my Lord in the manger of the ass;
I strengthened Moses through the water of Jordan;
I have been in the firmament with Mary Magdalen;
I have obtained the muse from the cauldron of Ceridwen;
I have been bard of the harp to Lleon of Lochlin;
I have been on the White Hill, in the court of Cynvelyn;
For a day and a year in stocks and fetters,
I have suffered for the Son of the Virgin.
I have been fostered in the land of the Deity,
I have been teacher to all intelligences,
I am able to instruct the whole universe,
I shall be until the day of doom on the face of the earth;
And it is not known whether my body is flesh or fish.

Taliesin.

The Retreat

HAPPY those early days, when I
　　Shined in my Angel-infancy!
Before I understood this place
Appointed for my second race,
Or taught my soul to fancy aught
But a white celestial thought:
When yet I had not walk'd above
A mile or two from my first Love,
And looking back—at that short space---
Could see a glimpse of His bright face:
When on some gilded cloud, or flow'r,
My gazing soul would dwell an hour,
And in those weaker glories spy
Some shadows of eternity:
Before I taught my tongue to wound
My Conscience with a sinful sound,
Or had the black art to dispense
A several sin to ev'ry sense,
But felt through all this fleshly dress
Bright shoots of everlastingness.

　O how I long to travel back,
And tread again that ancient track!
That I might once more reach that plain
Where first I left my glorious train;
From whence th' enlighten'd spirit sees
That shady City of Palm-trees.
But ah! my soul with too much stay
Is drunk, and staggers in the way!

Some men a forward motion love,
But I by backward steps would move;
And when this dust falls to the urn,
In that state I came, return.

Henry Vaughan.

Wonder ᔓ ᔓ ᔓ ᔓ

HOW like an Angel came I down!
   How bright were all things here!
When first among His works I did appear
  O how their Glory me did crown!
The world resembled his *Eternity*,
    In which my soul did walk;
  And every thing that I did see
    Did with me talk.

The skies in their magnificence,
    The lively, lovely air,
Oh how divine, how soft, how sweet, how fair!
  The stars did entertain my sense,
And all the works of God, so bright and pure,
    So rich and great did seem,
  As if they ever must endure
    In my esteem.

A native health and innocence
    Within my bones did grow,
And while my God did all his glories show,
  I felt a vigour in my sense

That was all Spirit. I within did flow
    With seas of life, like wine;
  I nothing in the world did know
    But 'twas divine.

Harsh ragged objects were concealed,
    Oppressions, tears and cries,
Sins, griefs, complaints, dissensions, weeping eyes
  Were hid, and only things revealed
Which heavenly Spirits and the Angels prize.
    The state of Innocence
  And bliss, not trades and poverties,
    Did fill my sense.

The streets were paved with golden stones,
    The boys and girls were mine,
Oh how did all their lovely faces shine!
    The sons of men were holy ones,
In joy and beauty they appeared to me,
    And every thing which here I found,
  While like an angel I did see,
    Adorned the ground.

Rich diamond and pearl and gold
    In every place was seen;
Rare splendours, yellow, blue, red, white and green
  Mine eyes did everywhere behold.
Great Wonders clothed with glory did appear,
    Amazement was my bliss,
  That and my wealth was everywhere;
    No joy to this!

Cursed and devised proprieties,
    With envy, avarice
And fraud, those fiends that spoil even Paradise,
  Flew from the splendour of mine eyes.
And so did hedges, ditches, limits, bounds,
    I dreamed not aught of those,
  But wandered over all men's grounds,
    And found repose.
  Proprieties themselves were mine,
    And hedges ornaments;

Walls, boxes, coffers, and their rich contents
  Did not divide my joys, but all combine.
Clothes, ribbons, jewels, laces, I esteemed
    My joys by others worn :
  For me they all to wear them seemed
    When I was born.
               Thomas Traherne.

Keep Innocency

LIKE an old battle, youth is wild
    With bugle and spear, and counter cry,
Fanfare and drummery, yet a child
Dreaming of that sweet chivalry
The piercing terror cannot see.

He, with a mild and serious eye
Along the azure of the years,
Sees the sweet pomp sweep hurtling by;
But he sees not death's blood and tears,
Sees not the plunging of the spears.

And all the strident horror of
Horse and rider in red defeat
Is only music fine enough
To lull him into slumber sweet
In fields where ewe and lambkin bleat.

O, if with such simplicity
Himself take arms and suffer war;
With beams his targe shall gilded be,
Tho' in the thickening gloom be far
The steadfast light of any star!

Tho' hoarse war's eagle on him perch,
Quickened with guilty lightnings,—there
It shall in vain for terror search,
Where a child's eyes 'neath bloody hair
Gaze purely thro' the dingy air.

And when the wheeling rout is spent,
Tho' in the heaps of slain he lie;
Or lonely in his last content;
Quenchless shall burn in secrecy
The flame Death knows his victors by.

Walter de la Mare

Highway, my Parnassus

HIGH way! since you my chief Parnassus be;
   And that my Muse, to some ears not unsweet,
  Tempers her words to trampling horses' feet
More oft than to a chamber-melody.
Now blessed you, bear onward blessed me

To her, where I my heart safe left shall meet;
   My Muse and I must you of duty greet
With thanks and wishes, wishing thankfully.
   Be you still fair, honoured by public heed;
By no encroachment wronged, nor time forgot;
   Nor blamed for blood, nor shamed for sinful deed;
And that you know I envy you no lot
   Of highest wish, I wish you so much bliss,—
   Hundreds of years you Stella's feet may kiss.
                              Sir P. Sidney.

That's the Way ∽ ∽ ∽

WHERE the pools are bright and deep,
   Where the grey trout lies asleep,
Up the river and over the lea,
That's the way for Billy and me.

Where the blackbird sings the latest,
Where the hawthorn blooms the sweetest,
Where the nestlings chirp and flee,
That's the way for Billy and me

Where the mowers mow the cleanest,
Where the hay lies thick and greenest,
There to track the homeward bee,
That's the way for Billy and me.

Where the hazel bank is steepest,
Where the shadows fall the deepest,
Where the clustering nuts fall free,
That's the way for Billy and me.

Why the boys should drive away
Little maidens from their play,
Or love to banter and fight so well,
That's the thing I never could tell.

But this I know, I love to play
Through the meadow, among the hay;
Up the water and over the lea,
That's the way for Billy and me.

James Hogg.

To the Morning

Satisfaction for Sleepe

WHAT succour can I hope the Muse will send
   Whose drowsiness hath wrong'd the Muses friend?
What hope *Aurora* to propitiate thee,
Unlesse the Muse sing my Apologie?
   O in that morning of my shame! when I
Lay folded up in sleepes captivity,
How at the sight did'st Thou draw back thine Eyes,
Into thy modest veyle? how did'st thou rise
Twice dy'd in thine own blushes, and did'st run
To draw the Curtaines, and awake the Sun?
Who rowzing his illustrious tresses came,
And seeing the loath'd object, hid for shame

His head in thy faire Bosome, and still hides
Mee from his Patronage ; I pray, he chides :
And pointing to dull *Morpheus*, bids me take
My owne *Apollo*, try if I can make
His *Lethe* be my *Helicon;* and see
If *Morpheus* have a Muse to wait on mee.
Hence 'tis my humble fancie findes no wings,
No nimble rapture starts to Heaven and brings
Enthusiasticke flames, such as can give
Marrow to my plumpe *Genius*, make it live
Drest in the glorious madnesse of a Muse,
Whose feet can walke the milky way, and chuse
Her starry Throne ; whose holy heats can warme
The grave, and hold up an exalted arme
To lift me from my lazy Urne, to climbe
Upon the stooping shoulders of old Time,
And trace Eternity—But all is dead,
All these delicious hopes are buried
In the deepe wrinckles of his angry brow,
Where mercy cannot find them : but ô thou
Bright Lady of the Morne, pitty doth lye
So warme in thy soft Brest it cannot dye.
Have mercy then, and when He next shall rise
O meet the angry God, invade his Eyes,
And stroake his radiant Cheekes ; one timely kisse
Will kill his anger, and revive my blisse.
So to the treasure of thy pearly deaw,
Thrice will I pay three Teares, to show how true
My griefe is ; so my wakefull lay shall knocke
At th' Orientall Gates ; and duly mocke
The early Larkes shrill Orizons, to be

An Anthem at the Dayes Nativitie.
And the same rosie-finger'd hand of thine,
That shuts Nights dying eyes, shall open mine.
  But thou, faint God of sleepe, forget that I
Was ever known to be thy votary.
No more my pillow shall thine Altar be,
Nor will I offer any more to thee
My selfe a melting sacrifice ; I'me borne
Againe a fresh Child of the Buxome Morne,
Heire of the Suns first Beames ; why threat'st thou so?
Why dost thou shake thy leaden Scepter ? goe,
Bestow thy Poppy upon wakefull woe,
Sicknesse, and sorrow, whose pale liddes ne're know
Thy downie finger, dwell upon their Eyes,
Shut in their Teares ; Shut out their miseries.

Richard Crashaw.

Phœbus, Arise !   ∽   ∽   ∽

PHŒBUS, arise !
  And paint the sable skies
With azure, white, and red ;
Rouse Memnon's mother from her Tithon's bed,
That she may thy career with roses spread ;
The nightingales thy coming each-where sing ;
Make an eternal spring !

Give life to this dark world which lieth dead;
Spread forth thy golden hair
In larger locks than thou wast wont before,
And emperor-like decore
With diadem of pearl thy temples fair:
Chase hence the ugly night
Which serves but to make dear thy glorious light.
This is that happy morn,
That day, long wishèd day
Of all my life so dark
(If cruel stars have not my ruin sworn
And fates not hope betray),
Which, only white, deserves
A diamond for ever should it mark:
This is the morn should bring into this grove
My Love, to hear and recompense my love.
Fair King, who all preserves,
But show thy blushing beams,
And thou two sweeter eyes
Shalt see than those which by Penèus' streams
Did once thy heart surprise:
Nay, suns, which shine so clear
As thou when two thou did to Rome appear.
Now, Flora, deck thyself in fairest guise:
If that ye, winds, would hear
A voice surpassing far Amphion's lyre,
Your stormy chiding stay;
Let Zephyr only breathe
And with her tresses play,
Kissing sometimes those purple ports of death.
The winds all silent are;

And Phœbus in his chair
Ensaffroning sea and air
Makes vanish every star:
Night like a drunkard reels
Beyond the hills to shun his flaming wheels:
The fields with flowers are deck'd in every hue,
The clouds bespangle with bright gold their blue:
Here is the pleasant place—
And everything, save Her, who all should grace.

William Drummond.

The Last Ride Together

I SAID—Then, dearest, since 'tis so,
  Since now at length my fate I know,
Since nothing all my love avails,
Since all my life seemed meant for, fails,
  Since this was written and needs must be—
My whole heart rises up to bless
Your name in pride and thankfulness!
Take back the hope you gave,—I claim
Only a memory of the same,
—And this beside, if you will not blame,
  Your leave for one more last ride with me.

My mistress bent that brow of hers,
Those deep dark eyes where pride demurs
When pity would be softening through,
Fixed me a breathing-while or two
  With life or death in the balance—Right!

The blood replenished me again :
My last thought was at least not vain.
I and my mistress, side by side
Shall be together, breathe and ride,
So one day more am I deified.
   Who knows but the world may end to-night?

Hush ! if you saw some western cloud
All billowy-bosomed, over-bowed
By many benedictions—sun's
And moon's and evening star's at once—
   And so, you, looking and loving best,
Conscious grew, your passion drew
Cloud, sunset, moonrise, star-shine too
Down on you, near and yet more near,
Till flesh must fade for heaven was here !—
Thus leant she and lingered—joy and fear !
   Thus lay she a moment on my breast.

Then we began to ride. My soul
Smoothed itself out, a long-cramped scroll
Freshening and fluttering in the wind.
Past hopes already lay behind.
   What need to strive with a life awry?
Had I said that, had I done this,
So might I gain, so might I miss.
Might she have loved me? just as well
She might have hated,—who can tell?
Where had I been now if the worst befell?
   And here we are riding, she and I.

Fail I alone, in words and deeds?
Why, all men strive and who succeeds?
We rode; it seemed my spirit flew,
Saw other regions, cities new,
   As the world rushed by on either side.
I thought, All labour, yet no less
Bear up beneath their unsuccess.
Look at the end of work, contrast
The petty Done the Undone vast,
This present of theirs with the hopeful past!
   I hoped she would love me.   Here we ride.

What hand and brain went ever paired?
What heart alike conceived and dared?
What act proved all its thought had been?
What will but felt the fleshly screen?
   We ride and I see her bosom heave.
There's many a crown for who can reach.
Ten lines, a statesman's life in each!
The flag stuck on a heap of bones,
A soldier's doing! what atones?
They scratch his name on the Abbey-stones.
   My riding is better, by your leave.

What does it all mean, poet? well,
Your brains beat into rhythm—you tell
What we felt only; you expressed
You hold things beautiful the best,
   And pace them in rhyme so, side by side.
Tis something, nay 'tis much—but then,
Have you yourself what's best for men?

Are you—poor, sick, old ere your time—
Nearer one whit your own sublime
Than we who never have turned a rhyme?
   Sing, riding's a joy! For me, I ride.

And you, great sculptor—so you gave
A score of years to Art, her slave,
And that's your Venus—whence we turn
To yonder girl that fords the burn!
   You acquiesce and shall I repine?
What, man of music, you, grown grey
With notes and nothing else to say,
Is this your sole praise from a friend,
"Greatly his opera's strains intend,
But in music we know how fashions end!"
   I gave my youth—but we ride, in fine.

Who knows what's fit for us? Had fate
Proposed bliss here should sublimate
My being; had I signed the bond—
Still one must lead some life beyond,
   —Have a bliss to die with, dim-descried.
This foot once planted on the goal,
This glory-garland round my soul,
Could I descry such? Try and test!
I sink back shuddering from the quest—
Earth being so good, would Heaven seem best?
   Now, Heaven and she are beyond this ride.

And yet—she has not spoke so long!
What if Heaven be, that, fair and strong

At life's best, with our eyes upturned
Whither life's flower is first discerned,
   We, fixed so, ever should so abide?
What if we still rode on, we two,
With life for ever old yet new,
Changed not in kind but in degree,
The instant made eternity,—
And Heaven just prove that I and she
   Ride, ride together, for ever ride?

Robert Browning.

Spring Without Her

SWEET spring, thou turn'st with all thy goodly traine,
Thy head with flames, thy mantle bright with flowers,
The zephyres curl the green locks of the plaine,
The clouds for joy in pearls weep down their showers.
Turn thou, sweet youth; but ah! my pleasant hours
And happy days with thee come not againe,
The sad memorials only of my paine
Do with thee turn, which turn my sweets to sours.
Thou art the same which still thou wert before,
Delicious, lusty, amiable, fair;
But she whose breath embalm'd thy wholesome air
Is gone; nor gold, nor gems can her restore.
Neglected Virtue! seasons go and come,
While thine, forgot, lie closed in a tomb.

William Drummond.

Fancy and Joy

ARE they shadows that we see?
   And can shadows pleasure give?
Pleasures only shadows be,
Cast by bodies we conceive,
And are made the things we deem
In those figures which they seem.

But these pleasures vanish fast,
Which by shadows are exprest;
Pleasures are not, if they last:
In their passing is their best.
Glory is more bright and gay
In a flash and so away.

Feed apace, then, greedy eyes
On the wonder you behold;
Take it sudden as it flies,
Though you take it not to hold.
When your eyes have done their part,
Thought must length it in the heart.

Samuel Daniel.

A Song of the Youths

LO! in the palace, lo! in the street,
   Beautiful beyond measure;
Yea, gods for glory, and women for sweet,
   The youths, the princes of pleasure!

Idle and crowned in the long day's sun,
　　Turbulent, passionate, sad ;
Full of the soul of the deed to be done,
　　Or the thought of the joy latest had ;
They walk their way through the crowds that run,
　　They pass through the crowds that part ;
And the women behold them, and each knows one,
　　How mighty he is in her heart.

Lo! in the palace . . .

They win with the vehemence of their souls,
　　With the swiftness of their fame ;
Their strong and radiant look controls,
　　And smiles the world to shame.
Their rule is large, and like fair lords,
　　They lavish a goodly treasure ;
They live of the joy the world affords
　　And they pay the world with pleasure.

One passes bright through the street down there,
　　Named and known of repute ;
And one hath a scandal of rich flowing hair,
　　And the musical tongue of a lute.
O the women, beholding, who thrill and say,
　　" While that one stays on the earth,
I can have in the secret of night or of day,
　　More delight than a man's life is worth."

O the woman that says in the midst of the crowd,
  " Beautiful, turbulent one,
Do I not know you through semblance and shroud,
  Even as I know the sun?
Burning, and swift, and divine you are ;
  But I have you all to treasure ;
Women may love you, but mine you are,
  And prince of the princes of pleasure."

Lo ! in the palace, lo ! in the street,
  Beautiful beyond measure;
Yea, gods for glory, and women for sweet,
  The youths, the princes of pleasure !

Arthur O'Shaughnessy.

The Merry Guide

ONCE in the wind of morning
  I ranged the thymy wold ;
The world-wide air was azure
  And all the brooks ran gold.

There through the dews beside me
  Behold a youth that trod,
With feathered cap on forehead,
  And poised a golden rod.

With mien to match the morning
  And gay delightful guise
And friendly brows and laughter
  He looked me in the eyes.

Oh whence, I asked, and whither?
  He smiled and would not say,
And looked at me and beckoned
  And laughed and led the way.

And with kind looks and laughter
  And nought to say beside
We two went on together,
  I and my happy guide.

Across the glittering pastures
  And empty upland still
And solitude of shepherds
  High in the folded hill,

By hanging woods and hamlets
  That gaze through orchards down
On many a windmill turning
  And far-discovered town,

With gay regards of promise
  And sure unslackened stride
And smiles and nothing spoken
  Led on my merry guide.

By blowing realms of woodland
  With sunstruck vanes afield
And cloud-led shadows sailing
  About the windy weald,

By valley-guarded granges
  And silver waters wide,
Content at heart I followed
  With my delightful guide.

And like the cloudy shadows
  Across the country blown
We two fare on for ever,
  But not we too alone.

With the great gale we journey
  That breathes from gardens thinned,
Borne in the drift of blossoms
  Whose petals throng the wind;

Buoyed on the heaven-heard whisper
  Of dancing leaflets whirled
From all the woods that autumn
  Bereaves in all the world.

And midst the fluttering legion
  Of all that ever died
I follow, and before us
  Goes the delightful guide,

With lips that brim with laughter
  But never once respond,
And feet that fly on feathers,
  And serpent-circled wand.

A. E. Housman.

Bunches of Grapes

"BUNCHES of grapes," says Timothy;
  "Pomegranates pink," says Elaine;
"A junket of cream and a cranberry tart
  For me," says Jane.

"Love-in-a-mist," says Timothy ;
"Primroses pale," says Elaine ;
"A nosegay of pinks and mignonette
    For me," says Jane.

"Chariots of gold," says Timothy ;
"Silvery wings," says Elaine ;
"A bumpity ride in a wagon of hay
    For me," says Jane.
Walter de la Mare.

Mont Blanc

Lines written in the Vale of Chamouni

THE everlasting universe of things
    Flows through the mind, and rolls its rapid waves,
Now dark—now glittering—now reflecting gloom—
Now lending splendour, where from secret springs
The source of human thought its tribute brings
Of waters,—with a sound but half its own,
Such as a feeble brook will oft assume
In the wild woods, among the mountains lone,
Where waterfalls around it leap for ever,
Where woods and winds contend, and a vast river
Over its rocks ceaselessly bursts and raves.

Thus thou, Ravine of Arve—dark, deep Ravine—
Thou many-coloured, many-voicèd vale,
Over whose pines, and crags, and caverns sail

Fast cloud-shadows and sunbeams : awful scene,
Where Power in likeness of the Arve comes down
From the ice-gulfs that gird his secret throne,
Bursting through these dark mountains like the flame
Of lightning through the tempest ;—thou dost lie,
Thy giant brood of pines around thee clinging,
Children of elder time, in whose devotion
The chainless winds still come and ever came
To drink their odours, and their mighty swinging
To hear—an old and solemn harmony ;
Thine earthly rainbows stretched across the sweep
Of the aethereal waterfall, whose veil
Robes some unsculptured image ; the strange sleep
Which when the voices of the desert fail
Wraps all in its own deep eternity ;—
Thy caverns echoing to the Arve's commotion,
A loud, lone sound no other sound can tame ;
Thou art pervaded with that ceaseless motion,
Thou art the path of that unresting sound—
Dizzy Ravine! and when I gaze on thee
I seem as in a trance sublime and strange
To muse on my own separate fantasy,
My own, my human mind, which passively
Now renders and receives fast influencings,
Holding an unremitting interchange
With the clear universe of things around ;
One legion of wild thoughts, whose wandering wings
Now float above thy darkness, and now rest
Where that or thou art no unbidden guest,

In the still cave of the witch Poesy,
Seeking among the shadows that pass by,
Ghosts of all things that are, some shade of thee,
Some phantom, some faint image ; till the breast
From which they fled recalls them, thou art there!

Some say that gleams of a remoter world
Visit the soul in sleep,—that death is slumber,
And that its shapes the busy thoughts outnumber
Of those who wake and live.—I look on high ;
Has some unknown omnipotence unfurled
The veil of life and death? or do I lie
In dream, and does the mightier world of sleep
Spread far around and inaccessibly
Its circles? For the very spirit fails,
Driven like a homeless cloud from steep to steep
That vanishes among the viewless gales !
Far, far above, piercing the infinite sky,
Mont Blanc appears,—still, snowy, and serene—
Its subject mountains their unearthly forms
Pile around it, ice and rock ; broad vales between
Of frozen floods, unfathomable deeps,
Blue as the overhanging heaven, that spread
And wind among the accumulated steeps ;
A desert peopled by the storms alone,
Save when the eagle brings some hunter's bone,
And the wolf tracks her there—how hideously
Its shapes are heaped around! rude, bare, and high,
Ghastly, and scarred, and riven.—Is this the scene
Where the old Earthquake-daemon taught her young

Ruin ? Were these their toys ? or did a sea
Of fire envelop once this silent snow ?
None can reply—all seems eternal now.
The wilderness has a mysterious tongue
Which teaches awful doubt, or faith so mild,
So solemn, so serene, that man may be,
But for such faith, with nature reconciled ;
Thou hast a voice, great Mountain, to repeal
Large codes of fraud and woe ; not understood
By all, but which the wise, and great, and good
Interpret, or make felt, or deeply feel.

The fields, the lakes, the forests, and the streams,
Ocean, and all the living things that dwell
Within the daedal earth ; lightning, and rain,
Earthquake, and fiery flood, and hurricane,
The torpor of the year when feeble dreams
Visit the hidden buds, or dreamless sleep
Holds every future leaf and flower ;—the bound
With which from that detested trance they leap ;
The works and ways of man, their death and birth,
And that of him and all that his may be ;
All things that move and breathe with toil and sound
Are born and die ; revolve, subside and swell.
Power dwells apart in its tranquillity,
Remote, serene, and inaccessible :
And *this*, the naked countenance of earth,
On which I gaze, even these primaeval mountains
Teach the adverting mind. The glaciers creep
Like snakes that watch their prey, from their far
    fountains,

Slow rolling on ; there, many a precipice,
Frost and the Sun in scorn of mortal power
Have piled : dome, pyramid, and pinnacle,
A city of death, distinct with many a tower
And wall impregnable of beaming ice.
Yet not a city, but a flood of ruin
Is there, that from the boundaries of the sky
Rolls its perpetual stream ; vast pines are strewing
Its destined path, or in the mangled soil
Branchless and shattered stand ; the rocks, drawn down
From yon remotest waste, have overthrown
The limits of the dead and living world,
Never to be reclaimed. The dwelling-place
Of insects, beasts, and birds, becomes its spoil ;
Their food and their retreat forever gone,
So much of life and joy is lost. The race
Of man flies far in dread ; his work and dwelling
Vanish, like smoke before the tempest's stream,
And their place is not known. Below, vast caves
Shine in the rushing torrents' restless gleam,
Which from those secret chasms in tumult welling
Meet in the vale, and one majestic River,
The breath and blood of distant lands, for ever
Rolls its loud waters to the ocean-waves,
Breathes its swift vapours to the circling air.

Mont Blanc yet gleams on high :—the power is there,
The still and solemn power of many sights,
And many sounds, and much of life and death.

In the calm darkness of the moonless nights,
In the lone glare of day, the snows descend
Upon that Mountain ; none beholds them there,
Nor when the flakes burn in the sinking sun,
Or the star-beams dart through them :—Winds
 contend
Silently there, and heap the snow with breath
Rapid and strong, but silently ! Its home
The voiceless lightning in these solitudes
Keeps innocently, and like vapour broods
Over the snow. The secret Strength of things
Which governs thought, and to the infinite dome
Of Heaven is as a law, inhabits thee !
And what were thou, and earth, and stars, and sea,
If to the human mind's imaginings
Silence and solitude were vacancy?
Percy Bysshe Shelley.

Inscription for a Fountain

THIS Sycamore, oft musical with bees,—
 Such tents the Patriarchs loved ! O long
  unharmed
May all its aged boughs o'er-canopy
The small round basin, which this jutting stone
Keeps pure from falling leaves ! Long may the
 Spring,
Quietly as a sleeping infant's breath,
Send up cold waters to the traveller
With soft and even pulse ! Nor ever cease

Yon tiny cone of sand its soundless dance,
Which at the bottom, like a Fairy's Page,
As merry and no taller, dances still,
Nor wrinkles the smooth surface of the Fount.
Here twilight is and coolness : here is moss,
A soft seat, and a deep and ample shade.
Thou may'st toil far and find no second tree.
Drink, Pilgrim, here ! Here rest ! and if thy heart
Be innocent, here too shalt thou refresh
Thy spirit, listening to some gentle sound,
Or passing gale or hum of murmuring bees !

Samuel Taylor Coleridge.

Men are Fools that wish to Die

HEY nonny no !
   Men are fools that wish to die !
Is't not fine to dance and sing
When the bells of death do ring ?
Is't not fine to swim in wine
And turn upon the toe
And sing hey nonny no,
When the winds blow and the seas flow ?
Hey nonny no !

Anonymous.

Earth for its Own Sake

  IS it not better, then, to be alone,
    And love Earth only for its earthly sake ?
By the blue rushing of the arrowy Rhone,
Or the pure bosom of its nursing lake,

Which feeds it as a mother who doth make
A fair but froward infant her own care,
Kissing its cries away as these awake ;—
Is it not better thus our lives to wear,
Than join the crushing crowd, doom'd to inflict or
    bear?

I live not in myself, but I become
Portion of that around me ; and to me
High mountains are a feeling, but the hum
Of human cities torture : I can see
Nothing to loathe in nature, save to be
A link reluctant in a fleshly chain,
Class'd among creatures, when the soul can flee,
And with the sky, the peak, the heaving plain
Of ocean, or the stars, mingle, and not in vain.

And thus I am absorb'd, and this is life ;
I look upon the peopled desert past,
As on a place of agony and strife,
Where, for some sin, to sorrow I was cast,
To act and suffer, but remount at last
With a fresh pinion ; which I feel to spring,
Though young, yet waxing vigorous, as the blast
Which it would cope with, on delighted wing,
Spurning the clay-cold bonds which round our
    being cling.

And when, at length, the mind shall be all free
From what it hates in this degraded form,
Reft of its carnal life, save what shall be
Existent happier in the fly and worm,—

When elements to elements conform,
And dust is as it should be, shall I not
Feel all I see, less dazzling, but more warm?
The bodiless thought? the Spirit of each spot?
Of which, even now, I share at times the immortal
    lot?

Are not the mountains, waves, and skies, a part
Of me and of my soul, as I of them?
Is not the love of these deep in my heart
With a pure passion? should I not contemn
All objects, if compared with these? and stem
A tide of suffering, rather than forego
Such feelings for the hard and worldly phlegm
Of those whose eyes are only turn'd below,
Gazing upon the ground, with thoughts which dare
    not glow?
Lord Byron

Fancy's Birth

TELL me where is fancy bred,
    Or in the heart, or in the head?
How begot, how nourished?
    Reply, reply.

It is engendered in the eyes,
With gazing fed; and fancy dies
In the cradle where it lies:
Let us all ring fancy's knell;
I'll begin it,—Ding, dong, bell.
    Ding, dong, bell.
Shakespeare.

Fancy   ∽   ∽   ∽

EVER let the Fancy roam,
  Pleasure never is at home:
At a touch sweet Pleasure melteth,
Like to bubbles when rain pelteth;
Then let winged Fancy wander
Through the thought still spread beyond her:
Open wide the mind's cage door,
She'll dart forth, and cloudward soar.
O sweet Fancy! let her loose;
Summer's joys are spoilt by use,
And the enjoying of the Spring
Fades as does its blossoming:
Autumn's red-lipp'd fruitage too,
Blushing through the mist and dew
Cloys with tasting: What do then?
Sit thee by the ingle, when
The sear faggot blazes bright,
Spirit of a winter's night;
When the soundless earth is muffled,
And the caked snow is shuffled
From the ploughboy's heavy shoon;
When the Night doth meet the Noon
In a dark conspiracy
To banish Even from her sky.
Sit thee there, and send abroad,
With a mind self-overawed,
Fancy, high-commission'd:—send her:
She has vassals to attend her:
She will bring, in spite of frost,

Beauties that the earth hath lost ;
She will bring thee, all together,
All delights of summer weather ;
All the buds and bells of May,
From dewy sward or thorny spray ;
All the heaped Autumn's wealth,
With a still, mysterious stealth :
She will mix these pleasures up
Like three fit wines in a cup,
And thou shalt quaff it :—thou shalt hear
Distant harvest-carols clear ;
Rustle of the reaped corn ;
Sweet birds antheming the morn :
And, in the same moment—hark !
'Tis the early April lark,
Or the rooks, with busy caw,
Foraging for sticks and straw.
Thou shalt, at one glance, behold
The daisy and the marigold ;
White-plumed lilies, and the first
Hedge-grown primrose that hath burst ;
Shaded hyacinth, alway
Sapphire queen of the mid-May ;
And every leaf, and every flower
Pearled with the self-same shower.
Thou shalt see the field-mouse peep
Meagre from its celled sleep ;
And the snake all winter-thin
Cast on sunny bank its skin ;
Freckled nest eggs thou shalt see
Hatching in the hawthorn-tree,

When the hen-bird's wing doth rest
Quiet on her mossy nest ;
Then the hurry and alarm
When the bee-hive casts its swarm ;
Acorns ripe down-pattering
While the autumn breezes sing.

Oh, sweet Fancy ! let her loose ;
Everything is spoilt by use :
Where's the cheek that doth not fade,
Too much gazed at ? Where's the maid
Whose lip mature is ever new ?
Where's the eye, however blue,
Doth not weary ? Where's the face
One would meet in every place ?
Where's the voice, however soft,
One would hear so very oft ?
At a touch sweet Pleasure melteth,
Like to bubbles when rain pelteth.
Let, then, winged Fancy find
Thee a mistress to thy mind :
Dulcet-eyed as Ceres' daughter,
Ere the god of Torment taught her
How to frown and how to chide ;
With a waist and with a side
White as Hebe's, when her zone
Slipt its golden clasp, and down
Fell her kirtle to her feet,
While she held the goblet sweet,
And Jove grew languid.—Break the mesh
Of the Fancy's silken leash ;

Quickly break her prison-string
And such joys as these she'll bring.—
Let the winged Fancy roam,
Pleasure never is at home.

John Keats.

July ∽ ∽ ∽

THE Kings come riding back from the Crusade,
   The purple Kings and all their mounted men ;
They fill the street with clamorous cavalcade :
   The Kings have broken down the Saracen.
Singing a great song of the eastern wars,
   In crimson ships across the sea they came,
With crimson sails and diamonded dark oars,
   That made the Mediterranean flash with flame.

And reading how, in that far month, the ranks
   Formed on the edge of the desert, armoured all,
   I wish to God that I had been with them
When the first Norman leapt upon the wall,
And Godfrey led the foremost of the Franks,
   And young lord Raymond stormed Jerusalem.

Hilaire Belloc.

To the Cuckoo ∽ ∽ ∽

O BLITHE New-comer ! I have heard,
   I hear thee and rejoice.
O Cuckoo ! shall I call thee Bird,
   Or but a wandering Voice ?

While I am lying on the grass
  Thy twofold shout I hear;
From hill to hill it seems to pass
  At once far off and near.

Though babbling only to the Vale,
  Of sunshine and of flowers,
Thou bringest unto me a tale
  Of visionary hours.

Thrice welcome, darling of the Spring!
  Even yet thou art to me
No Bird, but an invisible Thing,
  A voice, a mystery;

The same whom in my Schoolboy days
  I listened to; that Cry
Which made me look a thousand ways
  In bush, and tree, and sky.

To seek thee did I often rove
  Through woods and on the green;
And thou wert still a hope, a love;
  Still longed for, never seen.

And I can listen to thee yet;
  Can lie upon the plain
And listen, till I do beget
  That golden time again.

O blessèd Bird! the earth we pace
  Again appears to be
An unsubstantial, faery place;
  That is fit home for Thee!

William Wordsworth.

With Un-uplifted Eyes

MOST sweet it is with un-uplifted eyes
  To pace the ground, if path be there or none,
While a fair region round the traveller lies
Which he forbears again to look upon ;
Pleased rather with some soft ideal scene,
The work of Fancy, or some happy tone
Of meditation, slipping in between
The beauty coming and the beauty gone.
If Thought and Love desert us, from that day
Let us break off all commerce with the Muse :
With Thought and Love companions of our way,
Whate'er the senses take or may refuse,
The Mind's internal heaven shall shed her dews
Of inspiration on the humblest lay.

William Wordsworth.

The Prince and Spring

I LOVE the time of summer, when the steed
  Of the exulting chief prances before a gallant lord,
When the nimbly moving wave is covered with foam,
When the apple tree is transfigured with blossom,
And when the white shield is borne on my shoulder to the conflict.

Translated from *Howel ab Owain.*

From "Comus"

THERE is a gentle Nymph not far from hence,
   That with moist curb sways the smooth Severn stream:
Sabrina is her name, a virgin pure;
Whilom she was the daughter of Locrine,
That had the sceptre from his father Brute.
She, guiltless damsel, flying the mad pursuit
Of her enraged stepdame Gwendolen,
Commended her fair innocence to the flood
That stayed her flight with his cross-flowing course.
The water-nymphs, that in the bottom played,
Held up their pearled wrists, and took her in,
Bearing her straight to aged Nereus' hall;
Who, piteous of her woes, reared her lank head,
And gave her to his daughter to imbathe
In nectared lavers strewed with asphodel,
And through the porch and inlet of each sense
Dropt in ambrosial oils, till she revived,
And underwent a quick immortal change,
Made Goddess of the river. Still she retains
Her maiden gentleness, and oft at eve
Visits the herds along the twilight meadows,
Helping all urchin blasts, and ill-luck signs
That the shrewd meddling elf delights to make,
Which she with precious vialed liquors heals:
For which the shepherds at their festivals,
Carol her goodness loud in rustic lays,
And throw sweet garland wreaths into her stream
Of pansies, pinks, and gaudy daffodils.

John Milton.

The Nightingale

SING to me, sing, and sing again,
   My glad, great-throated nightingale:
Sing, as the good sun through the rain—
   Sing, as the home-wind in the sail!

Sing to me life, and toil, and time,
   O bugle of dawn, O flute of rest!
Sing, and once more, as in the prime
   There shall be nought but seems the best.

And sing me at the last of love:
   Sing that old magic of the May,
That makes the great world laugh and move
   As lightly as our dream to-day!

William Ernest Henley.

Roadways

ONE road leads to London,
   One road runs to Wales,
My road leads me seawards
   To the white dipping sails.
        One road leads to the river,
           As it goes singing slow;
        My road leads to shipping,
           Where the bronzed sailors go.

Leads me, lures me, calls me
  To salt green tossing sea;
A road without earth's road-dust
  Is the right road for me.
    A wet road heaving, shining,
      And wild with sea-gulls' cries,
    A mad salt sea-wind blowing
      The salt spray in my eyes.

My road calls me, lures me
  West, east, south, and north;
Most roads lead me homewards,
  My road leads me forth
    To add more miles to the tally
      Of grey miles left behind,
    In quest of that one beauty
      God put me here to find.
              John Masefield.

The Cheerful Horn
From "English County Songs,' Edited by
Lucy Broadwood and J. A. Fuller Maitland

The cheer-ful ârn he blaws in the marn, And
we'll a-'unt-in' goo; The cheer-ful ârn he
blaws in the marn, And we'll a-'unt-in' goo, And

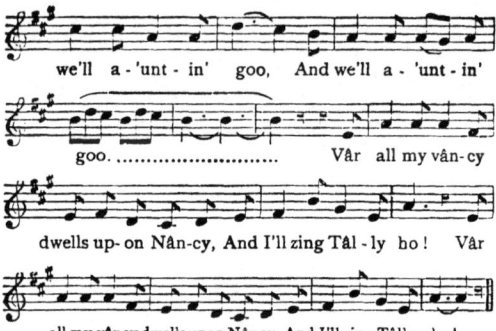

II

The vox jumps awer the 'edge zo 'igh,
    An' the 'ouns âll âtter un goo;
        Vâr all my vâncy, etc.

III

Then never despoise the soldjer lod,
    Thof 'is ztaition be boot low;
        Vâr all my vâncy, etc.

IV

Then push about the coop, my bwoys,
    An' we will wumwârds goo,
        Vâr all my vâncy, etc.

V

If you ax me the zenze of this zong vur to tell,
    Or the reäzon vur to zhow;
Woy, I doan't exacaly knoo, (*bis*)
    Vâr all my vâncy, etc.

In the Merry Month of May

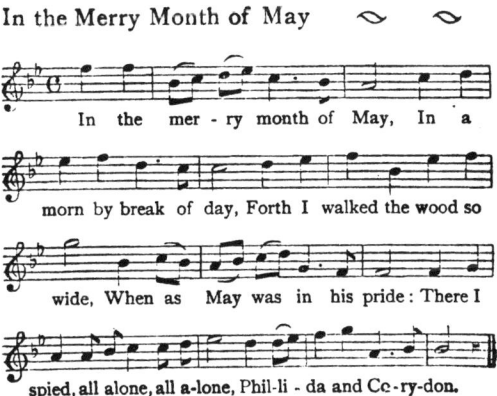

In the mer-ry month of May, In a morn by break of day, Forth I walked the wood so wide, When as May was in his pride: There I spied, all alone, all a-lone, Phil-li - da and Co-ry-don.

II

Much ado there was, God wot,
He would love and she would not.
She said "Never man was true."
He said "None was false to you."
He said he had loved too long,
She said love should have no wrong.

III

Corydon would have kissed her then,
She said maids should kiss no men
Till they did for good and all ;
Then she made the shepherd call
On all the Heavens, to witness truth
Never loved a truer youth.

IV

Thus with many a pretty oath,
Yea and Nay and Faith and Troth,
Such as silly shepherds use
When they will not Love abuse,
Love, which had been long deluded,
Was with kisses sweet concluded.

And Phillida with garlands gay
Was crowned the Lady of the May.

Nicholas Breton.

Early One Morning

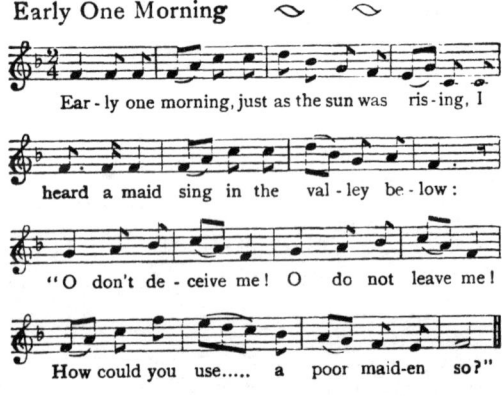

Ear-ly one morning, just as the sun was ris-ing, I heard a maid sing in the val-ley be-low: "O don't de-ceive me! O do not leave me! How could you use..... a poor maid-en so?"

II

O gay is the garland, fresh are the roses
I've culled from the garden to bind on thy brow:
    O don't deceive me, etc.

III

Remember the vows that you made to your Mary,
Remember the bower where you vow'd to be true :
    O don't deceive me, etc.

IV

Thus sang the poor maiden her sorrow bewailing,
Thus sang the poor maid in the valley below :
    O don't deceive me, etc.

La Fête des fous—La Prose de l'âne

O - ri - en - tis par - ti - bus   Ad - ven - tav - it
A - si - nus,   Pul-cher et for - tis - si - mus,
Sar - ci - nis ap - tis - si - mus.   Hez sire as - ne
car chan-tez,   Bel - le bou-che re - chig-nez, Vous au -
- rez du foin as - sez,   Et de l'avoine a plan-tez.

II

Lentus erat pedibus
Nisi foret baculus
Et eum in clunibus
Pungeret aculeus.
    Hez, sire asne, etc.

III

Ecce magnis auribus
Subjugalis filius
Asinus egregius
Asinorum dominus
    Hez, sire asne, etc.

IV

Saltu vincit hinnulos,
Damas et agricolos,
Super dromedarios
Velox madianeos.
    Hez, sire asne, etc.

V

Cum aristis hordeum
Comedit et carduum,
Triticum a palea
Segregat in area.
    Hez, sire asne, etc.

Amen dicas, asine,
Jam satur de gramine,
Amen, amen, itera
Aspernare vetera.
    Hez, sire asne, etc.

Drunken Sailor

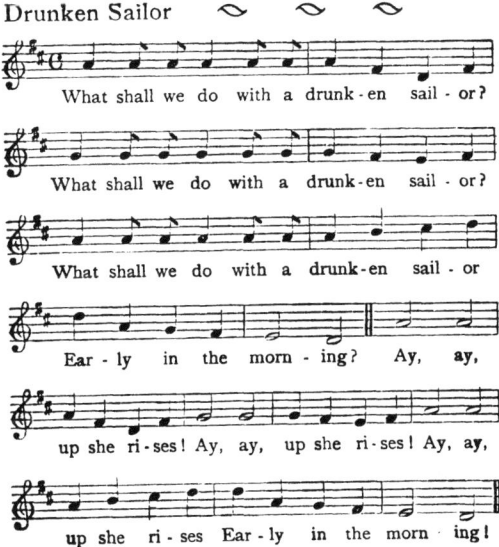

What shall we do with a drunk-en sail-or?
What shall we do with a drunk-en sail-or?
What shall we do with a drunk-en sail-or
Ear-ly in the morn-ing? Ay, **ay,**
up she ri-ses! Ay, ay, up she ri-ses! Ay, **ay,**
up she ri-ses Ear-ly in the morn-ing!

II

Stop his grog and make him sober,
Stop his grog and make him sober
Stop his grog and make him sober,
Early in the morning!
    Ay, ay, up she rises, etc.

III

Set him polishing up the brasswork,
Set him polishing up the brasswork,
Set him polishing up the brasswork,
Early in the morning!
    Ay, ay, up she rises, etc.

IV

That's what to do with a drunken sailor,
That's what to do with a drunken sailor,
That's what to do with a drunken sailor,
Early in the morning!

    Ay, ay, up she rises, etc.

My Collier Laddie

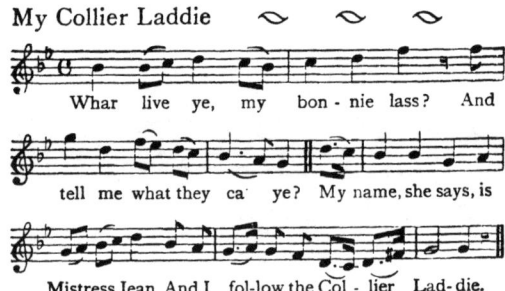

Whar live ye, my bonnie lass? And tell me what they ca' ye? My name, she says, is Mistress Jean, And I follow the Collier Laddie.

II

See ye not yon hills and dales,
    The sun shines on sae brawlie!
They a' are mine, and they shall be thine
    Gin ye leave your collier laddie.

III

Ye shall gang in gay attire,
    Weel buskit up sae gawdy;
And ane to wait on every hand,
    Gin ye leave your collier laddie.

IV

Though you had a' the sun shines on,
    And the earth conceals sae lowly,

I wad turn my back on you and it a',
  And embrace my collier laddie.

V

I can win my five-pennies in a day,
  And spen't at nicht fu' brawlie;
And make my bed in the collier's neuk,
  And lie down wi' my collier laddie.

VI

Love for love is the bargain for me,
  Tho' the wee cot-house should hauld me,
And the warld before me to win my bread,
  And fair fa' my collier laddie.   *Anonymous.*

The Lincolnshire Poacher

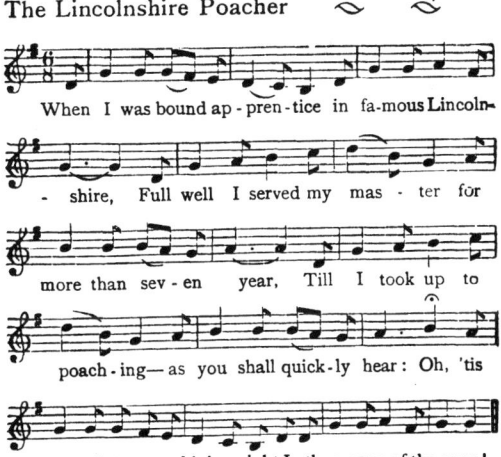

When I was bound ap-pren-tice in fa-mous Lincoln-shire, Full well I served my mas-ter for more than sev-en year, Till I took up to poach-ing— as you shall quick-ly hear: Oh, 'tis my delight on a shining night In the season of the year!

II

As me and my comrade were setting of a snare,
'Twas then we spied the gamekeeper, for him we did not care,
For we can wrestle and fight, my boys, and jump o'er anywhere.
    Oh, 'tis, etc.

III

As me and my comrade were setting four or five,
And taking on 'em up again we caught a hare alive,
We took the hare alive, my boys, and through the woods did steer.
    Oh, 'tis, etc.

IV

I threw him on my shoulder, and then we trudged home,
We took him to a neighbour's house and sold him for a crown,
We sold him for a crown, my boys, but I did not tell you where.
    Oh, 'tis, etc.

V

Success to every gentleman that lives in Lincolnshire,
Success to every poacher that wants to sell a hare,
Bad luck to every gamekeeper that will not sell his deer.
    Oh, 'tis, etc.

The Whale

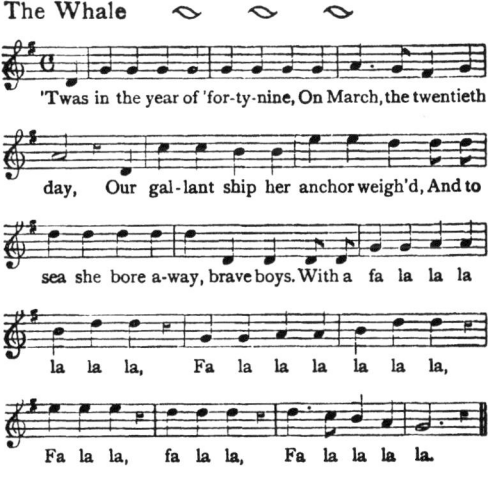

'Twas in the year of 'for-ty-nine, On March, the twentieth day, Our gal-lant ship her anchor weigh'd, And to sea she bore a-way, brave boys. With a fa la la la la la la, Fa la la la la la la, Fa la la, fa la la, Fa la la la la.

II

Old Blowhard was our captain's name,
  Our ship the "Lion" bold,
And we were bound to the North Country
  To face the frost and the cold,
    Brave boys, etc.

III

And when we came to that cold country
  Where the ice and the snow do lie,
Where there's ice and snow, and the great whales blow,
  And the daylight does not die,
    Brave boys, etc.

IV

Our mate went up to the topmast head
    With a spyglass in his hand:
"A whale, a whale, a whale," he cries,
    "And she spouts at every span,"
        Brave boys, etc.

V

Up jumped old Blowhard on the deck—
    And a clever little man was he—
"Overhaul, overhaul, let your maintackle fall,
    And launch your boat to sea,"
        Brave boys, etc.

VI

We struck that fish and away she flew
With a flourish of her tail;
But oh! and alas! we lost one man
And we did not catch that whale,
    Brave boys, etc.

VII

Now when the news to our captain came
He called up all his crew,
And for the losing of that man
He down his colours drew,
    Brave boys, etc.

VIII

Says he: "My men, be not dismayed
At the losing of one man,
For Providence will have his will,
Let man do what he can,"
    Brave boys, etc.

IX

Now the losing of that prentice boy
It grieved our captain sore,
But the losing of that great big whale
It grieved him a damned sight more.
  Brave boys, etc.

With a fa la la la la la la la
Fa la la la la la la
Fa la la fa la la
Fa la la la la.

Let the Bullgine Run

II

Oh, the "Marg'ret Evans" of the Blue Cross line,
  Ah ho, way-o, etc.
She's never a day behind her time,
  So clear the track, etc.
    Tibby hey, rig-a-jig, etc.

III

Oh, shake her, wake her before we're gone,
  Ah ho, way-o, etc.
Oh, fetch that girl with the blue dress on.
  So clear the track, etc.
    Tibby hey, rig-a-jig, etc.

Mowing Song

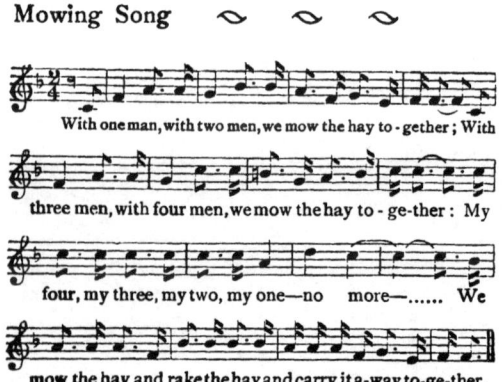

With one man, with two men, we mow the hay to-gether; With three men, with four men, we mow the hay to-ge-ther: My four, my three, my two, my one—no more—...... We mow the hay and rake the hay and carry it a-way to-ge-ther.

II

With five men, with six men, we mow the hay together;
With seven men, with eight men, we mow the hay together.
My eight, my seven, my six, my five, my four, my three, my two, my one, no more,
We mow the hay, and rake the hay, and carry it away together.

(*And so on, to a hundred, or until the singers shall cease.*)

Rum and Milk 〜 〜 〜

Air by Maud Aldis

Now, some may drink to la-dies fine, With painted cheeks and gowns of silk; But we will drink to dai-ry-maids, In pock-et mugs of rum and milk! O, 'tis up in the morning ear-ly When the dew is on the grass, And St. John's bell rings for matins, And St. Mary's rings for mass!

II

The merry skylarks soar and sing,
  And seem to Heaven very near—
Who knows what blessed inns they see,
  What holy drinking songs they hear?
    O, 'tis up in the morning early, etc.

III

The mushrooms may be priceless pearls
  A queen has lost beside the stream,
But rum is melted rubies when
  It turns the milk to golden cream!
    O, 'tis up in the morning early, etc.

Charles Dalmon.

My Little Pretty One

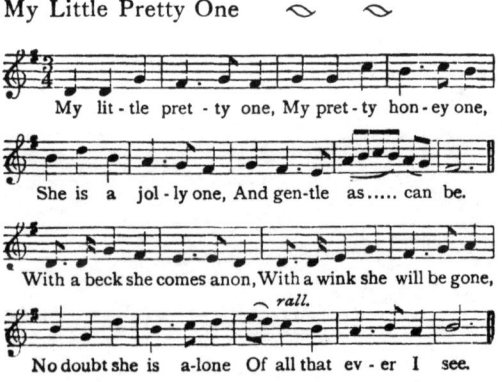

My little pretty one, My pretty honey one,
She is a jolly one, And gentle as..... can be.
With a beck she comes anon, With a wink she will be gone,
No doubt she is a-lone Of all that ever I see.

Marching Along

Words by Robert Browning
Air: "Lilliburlero"

Kentish Sir Byng stood for his King, Bidding the crop-headed
Hampden to hell, and his obsequies knell, Serve Hazelrig, Fiennes, and young

Parliament swing: And pressing a troop un-a-ble to stoop, And
Har-ry as well! England, good cheer! Ru-pert is near!

see the rogues flourish, and honest folk droop, Marched them a-long,
Kentish and Loy-alists, keep we not here. Marching a-long,

fif-ty score strong, Great-hearted gentlemen singing this song.
fif-ty score strong, Great-hearted gentlemen singing this song.

God for King Charles! Pym and his carles To the
Then, God for King Charles! Pym and his snarls To the

Dev-il that prompts 'em their treasonous parles! Cav-a-liers,
Dev-il that pricks on such pes-til-ent carles! Hold by the

up!.... Lips from the cup, Hands from the pas-ty, nor
right, you dou-ble your might; So on-ward to Nottingham

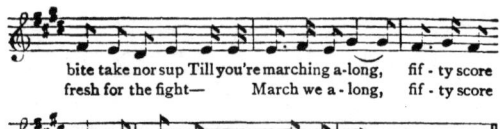

WAYSIDE REST

To Dianeme

SWEET, be not proud of those two eyes.
Which starlike sparkle in their skies;
Nor be you proud, that you can see
All hearts your captives,—yours, yet free.
Be you not proud of that rich hair
Which wantons with the love-sick air:
Whenas that ruby which you wear,
Sunk from the tip of your soft ear,
Will last to be a precious stone
When all your world of beauty's gone.
Robert Herrick

An Excelente Balade of Charitie

IN Virginè the sweltry sun 'gan sheene,
   And hot upon the mees did cast his ray;
The apple ripened from its paly green,
   And the soft pear did bend the leafy spray;
   The pied chelàndre sung the livelong day;
'Twas now the pride, the manhood of the year,
And eke the ground was dressed in its most neat
   aumere.

The sun was gleaming in the midst of day,
  Dead-still the air, and eke the welkin blue,
When from the sea arose in drear array
  A heap of clouds of sable sullen hue,
  Tne which full fast unto the woodland drew,
Hiding at once the sunnis beauteous face,
And the black tempest swelled, and gathered up apace.

Beneath a holm, fast by a pathway-side,
  Which did unto Saint Godwin's convent lead,
A hapless pilgrim moaning did abide,
  Poor in his view, ungentle in his weed,
  Long fillèd with the miseries of need.
Where from the hailstone could the beggar fly?
He had no houses there, nor any convent nigh.

Look in his clouded face, his sprite there scan;
  How woe-begone, how withered, sapless, dead!
Haste to thy church-glebe house, accursèd man!
  Haste to thy kiste, thy only sleeping bed.
  Cold as the clay which will grow on thy head
Is charity and love among high elves;
Knightnìs and barons live for pleasure and themselves.

The gathered storm is ripe; the big drops fall,
  The sun-burnt meadows smoke, and drink the rain;
The coming ghastness do the cattle 'pall,

And the full flocks are driving o'er the plain ;
Dashed from the clouds, the waters fly again ;
The welkin opes ; the yellow lightning flies,
And the hot fiery steam in the wide lowings dies.

List ! now the thunder's rattling noisy sound
　Moves slowly on, and then embollen clangs,
Shakes the high spire, and lost, expended, drowned,
　Still on the frighted ear of terror hangs ;
　The winds are up ; the lofty elmen swangs ;
Again the lightning and the thunder pours,
And the full clouds are burst at once in stony showers.

Spurring his palfrey o'er the watery plain,
　The Abbot of Saint Godwin's convent came ;
His chapournette was drentèd with the rain,
　And his pencte girdle met with mickle shame ;
　He backwards told his bede-roll at the same ;
The storm increases, and he drew aside,
With the poor alms-craver near to the holm to bide.

His cloak was all of Lincoln cloth so fine,
　With a gold button fastened near his chin,
His autremete was edged with golden twine,
　And his shoe's peak a loverde's might have been ;
　Full well it shewn he thoughten cost no sin.
The trammels of his palfrey pleased his sight,
For the horse-milliner his head with roses dight.

"An alms, sir priest!" the drooping pilgrim said,
   "Oh! let me wait within your convent door,
Till the sun shineth high above our head,
   And the loud tempest of the air is o'er.
   Helpless and old am I, alas! and poor.
No house, no friend, no money in my pouch,
All that I call my own is this my silver crouche."

"Varlet!" replied the Abbot, "cease your din;
   This is no season alms and prayers to give,
My porter never lets a beggar in;
   None touch my ring who not in honour live."
   And now the sun with the black clouds did strive,
And shedding on the ground his glaring ray;
The abbot spurred his steed, and eftsoons rode away.

Once more the sky was black, the thunder rolled,
   Fast running o'er the plain a priest was seen;
Not dight full proud, not buttoned up in gold,
   His cope and jape were grey, and eke were clean;
   A limitour he was of order seen;
And from the pathway-side then turnèd he,
Where the poor beggar lay beneath the elmen tree.

"An alms, sir priest!" the drooping pilgrim said,
   "For sweet Saint Mary and your order sake."
The limitour then loosened his pouch-thread,
   And did there out a groat of silver take:
   The needy pilgrim did for halline shake,

" Here, take this silver, it may ease thy care,
We are God's stewards all, naught of our own we
    bear.

" But ah! unhappy pilgrim, learn of me.
  Scathe any give a rent-roll to their Lord ;
Here, take my semi-cope, thou'rt bare, I see,
        'Tis thine ; the saints will give me my reward."
      He left the pilgrim, and his way aborde.
Virgin and holy saint, who sit in gloure,
Or give the mighty will, or give the good men
    power. *Thomas Chatterton.*

Song

COME, O come, my life's delight,
   Let me not in languor pine !
Love loves no delay ; thy sight,
   The more enjoyed, the more divine :
O come, and take from me
The pain of being deprived of thee !

Thou all sweetness dost enclose,
   Like a little world of bliss.
Beauty guards thy looks : the rose
   In them pure and eternal is.
Come then, and make thy flight
As swift to me as heavenly light.
                    Thomas Campion.

To His Coy Mistress

HAD we but world enough and time,
This coyness, lady, were no crime.
We would sit down and think which way
To walk, and pass our long love's day.
Thou by the Indian Ganges' side
Shouldst rubies find : I by the tide
Of Humber would complain. I would
Love you ten years before the Flood.
And you should, if you please, refuse
Till the conversion of the Jews.
My vegetable love should grow
Vaster than empires and more slow.
An hundred years should go to praise
Thine eyes, and on thy forehead gaze ;
Two hundred to adore each breast,
But thirty thousand to the rest ;
An age at least to every part,
And the last age should show your heart.
For, lady, you deserve this state,
Nor would I love at lower rate.

But at my back I always hear
Time's wingèd chariot hurrying near,
And yonder all before us lie
Deserts of vast eternity.
Thy beauty shall no more be found,
Nor in thy marble vault shall sound
My echoing song ; then worms shall try
That long-preserved virginity,

And your quaint honour turn to dust,
And into ashes all my lust.
The grave's a fine and private place,
But none, I think, do there embrace.
  Now, therefore, while the youthful hue
Sits on thy skin like morning dew,
And while thy willing soul transpires
At every pore with instant fires,
Now let us sport us while we may ;
And now, like amorous birds of prey,
Rather at once our time devour,
Than languish in his slow-chapped power !
Let us roll all our strength and all
Our sweetness up into one ball :
And tear our pleasures with rough strife,
Thorough the iron gates of life !
Thus, though we cannot make our sun
Stand still, yet we will make him run.
Andrew Marvell.

Waly, Waly ◡ ◡ ◡

O WALY, waly, up the bank,
  O waly, waly, doun the brae,
And waly, waly, yon burn-side,
  Where I and my love were wont to gae !
I lean'd my back unto an aik,
  I thocht it was a trustie tree,
But first it bow'd and syne it brak :—
  Sae my true love did lichtlie me.

O waly, waly, but love be bonnie
  A little while when it is new !
But when 'tis old, it waxeth cauld,
  And fadeth awa' like the morning dew.
O wherefore should I busk my heid,
  O wherefore should I kame my hair?
For my true love has me forsook,
  And says he'll never lo'e me mair.

Noo Arthur's Seat sall be my bed,
  The sheets sall ne'er be press'd by me ;
Saint Anton's well sall be my drink ;
  Since my true love's forsaken me.
Martinmas wind, when wilt thou blaw,
  And shake the green leaves off the tree?
O gentle death, when wilt thou come?
  For of my life I am wearie.

'Tis not the frost that freezes fell,
  Nor blawing snaw's inclemencie,
'Tis not sic cauld that makes me cry ;
  But my love's heart grown cauld to me.
But when we cam' in by Glasgow toun,
  We were a comely sicht to see ;
My love was clad in the black velvet,
  An' I mysel' in cramasie.

But had I wist before I kiss'd
  That love had been so ill to win,
I'd lock'd my heart in a case o' goud,
  And pinn'd it wi' a siller pin.

Oh, oh! if my young babe were born,
  And set upon the nurse's knee;
And I mysel' were dead and gane,
  And the green grass growing over me.
                                    Anonymous.

Farewell to Arms

HIS golden locks time hath to silver turned;
  O time too swift, O swiftness never ceasing!
His youth 'gainst time and age hath ever spurned,
  But spurned in vain; youth waneth by increasing:
Beauty, strength, youth, are flowers but fading seen;
Duty, faith, love, are roots, and ever green.

His helmet now shall make a hive for bees,
  And, lovers' sonnets turned to holy psalms,
A man-at-arms must now serve on his knees,
  And feed on prayers, which are age his alms:
But though from court to cottage he depart,
His saint is sure of his unspotted heart.

And when he saddest sits in homely cell,
  He'll teach his swains this carol for a song,—
"Blessed be the hearts that wish my sovereign well,
  Cursed be the souls that think her any wrong."
Goddess, allow this aged man his right,
To be your beadsman now that was your knight.
                                    George Peele.

Sir Patrick Spens

THE king sits in Dunfermline town,
    Drinking the blude-red wine:
"O whar will I get guid sailor
    To sail this ship of mine?"

Up and spake an eldern knight,
    Sat at the king's right knee:
"Sir Patrick Spens is the best sailor
    That sails upon the sea."

The king has written a braid letter,
    And signed it wi' his hand,
And sent it to Sir Patrick Spens,
    Was walking on the sand.

The first line that Sir Patrick read,
    A loud laugh laughed he;
The next line that Sir Patrick read,
    The tear blinded his ee.

"O wha is this has done this deed,
    This ill deed done to me,
To send me out this time o' the year,
    To sail upon the sea?

"Mak haste, mak haste, my mirry men all,
    Our guid ship sails the morne:"
"O say na sae, my master dear,
    For I fear a deadlie storme.

"Late, late, yestreen I saw the new moone
  Wi' the old moone in her arme,
And I fear, I fear, my dear master,
  That we will come to harme."

O our Scots nobles were right laith
  To weet their cork-heeled shoon;
But lang ere a' the play were playd,
  Their hats they swam aboon.

O lang, lang may their ladies sit,
  Wi' their fans into their hand,
Or ere they see Sir Patrick Spens
  Come sailing to the land.

O lang, lang may the ladies stand,
  Wi' their gold kaims in their hair,
Waiting for their ain dear lords,
  For they'll see them na mair.

Half owre, half owre to Aberdour,
  It's fifty fathom deep,
And there lies good Sir Patrick Spens,
  Wi' the Scots lords at his feet.

Anonymous.

Song

FAIN would I change that note
  To which fond love hath charmed me
Long, long to sing by rote,
  Fancying that that harmed me:

Yet when this thought doth come,
"Love is the perfect sum
  Of all delight,"
I have no other choice
Either for pen or voice
  To sing or write.

O love, they wrong thee much
  That say, thy sweet is bitter,
When thy rich fruit is such
  As nothing can be sweeter.
Fair house of joy and bliss,
Where truest pleasure is,
  I do adore thee;
I know thee what thou art,
I serve thee with my heart,
  And fall before thee.

Anonymous.

Prothalamion

CALM was the day, and through the trembling air
  Sweet-breathing Zephyrus did softly play—
A gentle spirit, that lightly did delay
Hot Titan's beams, which then did glister fair;
When I (whom sullen care,
Through discontent of my long fruitless stay
In princes' court, and expectation vain
Of idle hopes, which still do fly away
Like empty shadows, did afflict my brain)
Walk'd forth to ease my pain
Along the shore of silver-streaming Thames

Whose rutty bank, the which his river hems,
Was painted all with variable flowers,
And all the meads adorn'd with dainty gems
Fit to deck maidens' bowers,
And crown their paramours
Against the bridal day, which is not long:
    Sweet Thames! run softly, till I end my song.

There in a meadow by the river's side
A flock of nymphs I chancèd to espy,
All lovely daughters of the flood thereby,
With goodly greenish locks all loosed untied,
As each had been a bride;
And each one had a little wicker basket
Made of fine twigs, entrailèd curiously,
In which they gather'd flowers to fill their flasket,
And with fine fingers cropt full feateously
The tender stalks on high.
Of every sort which in that meadow grew
They gather'd some; the violet, pallid blue,
The little daisy that at evening closes,
The virgin lily and the primrose true:
With store of vermeil roses,
To deck their bridegrooms' posies
Against the bridal day, which was not long:
    Sweet Thames! run softly, till I end my song.

With that I saw two swans of goodly hue
Come softly swimming down along the lee;
Two fairer birds I yet did never see;

The snow which doth the top of Pindus strow
Did never whiter show,
Nor Jove himself, when he a swan would be
For love of Leda, whiter did appear ;
Yet Leda was (they say) as white as he,
Yet not so white as these, nor nothing near ;
So purely white they were
That even the gentle stream, the which them bare,
Seem'd foul to them, and bade his billows spare
To wet their silken feathers, lest they might
Soil their fair plumes with water not so fair,
And mar their beauties bright
That shone as Heaven's light
Against their bridal day, which was not long :
   Sweet Thames ! run softly, till I end my song.

Eftsoons the nymphs, which now had flowers their fill,
Ran all in haste to see that silver brood
As they came floating on the crystal flood ;
Whom when they saw, they stood amazèd still
Their wondering eyes to fill ;
Them seem'd they never saw a sight so fair
Of fowls, so lovely, that they sure did deem
Them heavenly born, or to be that same pair
Which through the sky draw Venus' silver team ;
For sure they did not seem
To be begot of any earthly seed,
But rather angels, or of angels' breed ;
Yet were they bred of summer's heat, they say,

In sweetest season, when each flower and weed
The earth did fresh array ;
So fresh they seem'd as day,
Even as their bridal day, which was not long :
    Sweet Thames ! run softly, till I end my song.

Then forth they all out of their baskets drew
Great store of flowers, the honour of the field,
That to the sense did fragrant odours yield,
All which upon those goodly birds they threw
And all the waves did strew,
That like old Peneus' waters they did seem,
When down along by pleasant Tempe's shore,
Scatter'd with flowers, through Thessaly they
    stream,
That they appear, through lilies' plenteous store,
Like a bride's chamber-floor.
Two of those nymphs meanwhile two garlands
    bound
Of freshest flowers which in that mead they found,
The which presenting all in trim array,
Their snowy foreheads there withal they crown'd ;
Whilst one did sing this lay
Prepared against that day,
Against that bridal day, which was not long :
    Sweet Thames ! run softly, till I end my song.

" Ye gentle birds ! the world's fair ornament,
And Heaven's glory, whom this happy hour
Doth lead unto your lovers' blissful bower,

Joy may you have, and gentle hearts content
Of your love's complement;
And let fair Venus, that is queen of love,
With her heart-quelling son upon you smile,
Whose smile, they say, hath virtue to remove
All love's dislike, and friendship's faulty guile
For ever to assoil.
Let endless peace your steadfast hearts accord,
And blessed plenty wait upon your board;
And let your bed with pleasures chaste abound,
That fruitful issue may to you afford,
Which may your foes confound,
And make your joys redound
Upon your bridal day, which is not long:
   Sweet Thames! run softly, till I end my song."

So ended she; and all the rest around
To her redoubled that her under song,
Which said their bridal day should not be long:
And gentle Echo from the neighbour ground
Their accents did resound.
So forth those joyous birds did pass along
Adown the lee that to them murmur'd low,
As he would speak but that he lack'd a tongue,
Yet did by signs his glad affection show,
Making his stream run slow.
And all the fowl which in his flood did dwell
'Gan flock about these twain, that did excel
The rest, so far as Cynthia doth shend
The lesser stars. So they, enrangèd well,

Did on those two attend,
And their best service lend
Against their wedding day, which was not long :
    Sweet Thames ! run softly, till I end my song.

At length they all to merry London came,
To merry London, my most kindly nurse,
That to me gave this life's first native source,
Though from another place I take my name,
An house of ancient fame :
There when they came, whereas those bricky towers
The which on Thames broad aged back do ride,
Where now the studious lawyers have their bowers,
There whilome wont the Templar-knights to bide,
Till they decay'd through pride ;
Next whereunto there stands a stately place,
Where oft I gainèd gifts and goodly grace
Of that great lord, which therein wont to dwell,
Whose want too well now feels my friendless case;
But ah ! here fits not well
Old woes, but joys to tell
Against the bridal day, which is not long :
    Sweet Thames ! run softly, till I end my song.

Yet therein now doth lodge a noble peer,
Great England's glory and the world's wide wonder,
Whose dreadful name late thro' all Spain did thunder,
And Hercules' two pillars standing near
Did make to quake and fear :
Fair branch of honour, flower of chivalry !
That fillest England with thy triumph's fame,
Joy have thou of thy noble victory,

And endless happiness of thine own name
That promiseth the same;
That through thy prowess and victorious arms
Thy country may be freed from foreign harms,
And great Eliza's glorious name may ring
Through all the world, fill'd with thy wide alarms
Which some brave Muse may sing
To ages following,
Upon the bridal day, which is not long :
   Sweet Thames ! run softly, till I end my song.

From those high towers this noble lord issùing
Like radiant Hesper, when his golden hair
In th' ocean billows he hath bathèd fair,
Descended to the river's open viewing
With a great train ensuing.
Above the rest were goodly to be seen
Two gentle knights of lovely face and feature,
Beseeming well the bower of any queen,
With gifts of wit and ornaments of nature
Fit for so goodly stature,
That like the twins of Jove they seem'd in sight
Which deck the baldric of the Heavens bright ;
They two, forth pacing to the river's side,
Received those two fair brides, their love's delight;
Which, at th' appointed tide,
Each one did make his bride
Against their bridal day, which is not long :
   Sweet Thames ! run softly, till I end my song.
                           Edmund Spenser.

Ode to Psyche

O GODDESS! hear these tuneless numbers, wrung
  By sweet enforcement and remembrance dear,
And pardon that thy secrets should be sung,
  Even into thine own soft-conched ear:
Surely I dreamt to-day, or did I see
  The winged Psyche with awaken'd eyes?
I wander'd in a forest thoughtlessly,
  And, on the sudden, fainting with surprise,
Sat two fair creatures, couched side by side
  In deepest grass, beneath the whispering roof
  Of leaves and trembled blossoms, where there ran
    A brooklet, scarce espied:
'Mid hush'd, cool-rooted flowers fragrant-eyed,
  Blue, silver-white, and budded Tyrian,
They lay calm-breathing on the bedded grass;
  Their arms embraced, and their pinions too;
  Their lips touch'd not, but had not bade adieu,
As if disjoined by soft-handed slumber,
And ready still past kisses to outnumber
  At tender eye-dawn of aurorean love:
    The winged boy I knew;
  But who wast thou, O happy, happy dove?
    His Psyche true!

O latest-born and loveliest vision far
  Of all Olympus' faded hierarchy!
Fairer than Phœbe's sapphire-region'd star,
  Or Vesper, amorous glow-worm of the sky;

Fairer than these, though temple thou hast none
    Nor altar heap'd with flowers;
Nor virgin-choir to make delicious moan
    Upon the midnight hours;
No voice, no lute, no pipe, no incense sweet
    From chain-swung censer teeming;
No shrine, no grove, no oracle, no heat
    Of pale-mouth'd prophet dreaming.
O brightest! though too late for antique vows,
    Too, too late for the fond believing lyre,
When holy were the haunted forest boughs,
    Holy the air, the water, and the fire;
Yet even in these days so far retired
    From happy pieties, thy lucent fans,
    Fluttering among the faint Olympians,
I see, and sing, by my own eyes inspired.
    So let me be thy choir, and make a moan
        Upon the midnight hours;
Thy voice, thy lute, thy pipe, thy incense sweet
    From swinged censer teeming:
Thy shrine, thy grove, thy oracle, thy heat
    Of pale-mouth'd prophet dreaming.

Yes, I will be thy priest, and build a fane
    In some untrodden region of my mind,
Where branched thoughts, new-grown with pleasant pain,
    Instead of pines shall murmur in the wind:
Far, far around shall those dark-cluster'd trees
    Fledge the wild-ridged mountains steep by steep;
And there by zephyrs, streams, and birds, and bees,

The moss-lain Dryads shall be lull'd to sleep;
And in the midst of this wide quietness
   A rosy sanctuary will I dress
With the wreath'd trellis of a working brain,
   With buds, and bells, and stars without a name,
With all the gardener Fancy e'er could feign,
   Who breeding flowers, will never breed the same:
And there shall be for thee all soft delight
   That shadowy thought can win,
A bright torch, and a casement ope at night,
   To let the warm Love in!
John Keats.

Willy Drowned in Yarrow

DOUN in yon garden sweet and gay
   Where bonnie grows the lily,
I heard a fair maid sighing say
   "My wish be wi' sweet Willie!

"Willie's rare, and Willie's fair,
   And Willie's wondrous bonny;
And Willie hecht to marry me
   Gin e'er he married ony.

"O gentle wind, that bloweth south,
   From where my Love repaireth,
Convey a kiss frae his dear mouth
   And tell me how he fareth!

"O tell sweet Willie to come doun
    And hear the mavis singing,
And see the birds on ilka bush
    And leaves around them hinging.

"The lav'rock there, wi' her white breist
    And gentle throat sae narrow;
There's sport eneuch for gentlemen
    On Leader haughs and Yarrow.

"O Leader haughs are wide and braid
    And Yarrow haughs are bonny;
There Willie hecht to marry me
    If e'er he married ony.

"But Willie's gone, whom I thought on,
    And does not hear me weeping;
Draws many a tear frae true love's e'e
    When other maids are sleeping.

"Yestreen I made my bed fu' braid,
    The night I'll mak' it narrow,
For a' the live-lang winter night
    I lie twinned o' my marrow.

"O came ye by yon water-side?
    Pou'd you the rose or lily?
Or came you by yon meadow green,
    Or saw you my sweet Willie?"

She sought him up, she sought him doun,
  She sought him braid and narrow ;
Syne, in the cleaving o' a craig,
  She found him drown'd in Yarrow !

Anonymous.

Sae Merry as We Twa Ha'e Been

A LASS that was laden wi' care
  Sat heavily under yon thorn ;
I listen'd a while for to hear,
  When thus she began for to mourn—
Whene'er my dear shepherd was there,
  The birds did melodiously sing,
And cold nipping winter did wear,
  A face that resembled the spring.
    Sae merry as we twa ha'e been,
      Sae merry as we twa ha'e been ;
    My heart is like for to break,
      When I think on the days we ha'e seen.

Our flocks feeding close by our side,
  He gently pressing my hand,
I viewed the wide world in its pride,
  And laugh'd at the pomp of command !
My dear, he would oft to me say,
  What makes you hard-hearted to me ?
Oh, why do you thus turn away,
  From him who is dying for thee ?

But now he is far from my sight,
   Perhaps a deceiver may prove,
Which makes me lament day and night,
   That ever I granted my love.
At eve, when the rest of the folk
   Are merrily seated to spin,
I set myself under an oak,
   And heavily sigh for him.

Anonymous.

Upon two greene Apricockes sent to Cowley by Sir Crashaw

TAKE these, times tardy truants, sent by me,
   To be chastis'd (sweet friend) and chide by thee.
Pale sons of our *Pomona!* whose wan cheekes
Have spent the patience of expecting weekes,
Yet are scarce ripe enough at best to show
The redd, but of the blush to thee they ow.
By thy comparrison they shall put on
More summer in their shames reflection,
Than ere the fruitfull *Phœbus* flaming kisses
Kindled on their cold lips. O had my wishes
And the deare merits of your Muse, their due,
The yeare had found some fruit early as you;
Ripe as those rich composures time computes
Blossoms, but our blest tast confesses fruits.
How does thy April-Autumne mocke these cold
Progressions 'twixt whose termes poor time grows
   old?

With thee alone he weares no beard, thy braine
Gives him the morning worlds fresh gold againe.
'Twas only Paradice, 'tis onely thou,
Whose fruit and blossoms both blesse the same bough.
Proud in the patterne of thy pretious youth,
Nature (methinks) might easily mend her growth.
Could she in all her births but coppie thee,
Into the publick yeares proficiencie,
No fruit should have the face to smile on thee,
(Young master of the worlds maturitie)
But such whose sun-borne beauties what they borrow
Of beames to day, pay back againe to morrow,
Nor need be double-gilt. How then must these,
Poore fruites looke pale at thy Hesperides !
Faine would I chide their slownesse, but in their
Defects I draw mine owne dull character.
Take them, and me in them acknowledging,
How much my summer waites upon thy spring.
Richard Crashaw.

My Lady Cometh   ◇   ◇   ◇

HYD, Absolon, thy gilte tresses clere ;
    Ester, ley thou thy meknesse al adoun ;
Hyd, Jonathas, al thy frendly manere ;
Penalopee, and Marcia Catoun,
Mak of your wyfhod no comparisoun ;
Hyde ye your beautes, Isoude and Eleyne ;
My lady cometh, that al this may disteyne.

Thy faire body, lat hit nat appere,
Lavyne; and thou, Lucresse of Rome toun,
And Polixene, that boghten love so dere,
And Cleopatre, with al thy passioun,
Hyde ye your trouthe of love and your renoun;
And thou, Tisbe, that hast of love swich peyne;
My lady cometh, that al this may disteyne.

Herro, Dido, Laudomia, alle y-fere,
And Phyllis, hanging for thy Demophoun,
And Canace, espyed thy chere,
Ysiphile, betraysed with Jasoun,
Maketh of your trouthe neyther boost ne soun;
Nor Ypermistre or Adriane, ye tweyne;
My lady cometh, that al this may disteyne.
Geoffrey Chaucer.

La Belle Dame sans Mercy

O WHAT can ail thee, knight-at-arms,
    Alone and palely loitering?
The sedge has wither'd from the lake,
    And no birds sing.

O what can ail thee, knight-at-arms,
    So haggard and so woe-begone?
The squirrel's granary is full,
    And the harvest's done.

I see a lily on thy brow,
    With anguish moist and fever dew,
And on thy cheek a fading rose
    Fast withereth too.

I met a lady in the meads,
    Full beautiful—a faery's child,
Her hair was long, her foot was light,
    And her eyes were wild.

I made a garland for her head,
    And bracelets too, and fragrant zone ;
She look'd at me as she did love,
    And made sweet moan.

I set her on my pacing steed,
    And nothing else saw all day long,
For sideways would she lean, and sing
    A faery's song.

She found me roots of relish sweet,
    And honey wild, and manna dew,
And sure in language strange she said—
    "I love thee true!"

She took me to her elfin grot,
    And there she wept and sigh'd full sore,
And there I shut her wild, wild eyes
    With kisses four.

And there she lulled me asleep,
    And there I dream'd—ah! woe betide !
The latest dream I ever dream'd
    On the cold hill's side.

I saw pale kings and princes too,
    Pale warriors, death-pale were they all ;
They cried—"La Belle Dame sans Merci
    Hath thee in thrall!"

I saw their starved lips in the gloam,
   With horrid warning gaped wide,
And I awoke and found me here,
   On the cold hill's side.

And this is why I sojourn here,
   Alone and palely loitering,
Though the sedge is wither'd from the lake,
   And no birds sing.

John Keats.

Young John and his True Sweetheart

A FAIR maid sat at her bower-door,
   Wringing her lily hands;
And by it came a sprightly youth
   Fast tripping o'er the strands.

"Where gang ye, young John," she says,
   "Sae early in the day?
It gars me think by your fast trip,
   Your journey's far away."

He turn'd about wi' an angry look,
   And said, "What's that to thee?
I'm gaen' to see a lovely may
   That's fairer far than ye."

"Now hae you played me this, fause love,
   In simmer, 'mid the flowers?
I sall repay ye back again
   In winter, 'mid the showers.

" But again, dear love, and again, dear love,
   Will ye not turn again?
For as ye look to ither women
   Sall I to ither men."

" O make your choice o' whom you please,
   For I my choice will have;
I've chosen a fairer may than thee,
   I never will deceive."

She's kilted up her claithing fine,
   And after him gaed she;
But aye he said, " Turn back, turn back,
   Nae further gang wi' me!"

" But again, dear love, and again, dear love,
   Will ye never love me again?
Alas! for loving you sae weel,
   And you nae me again!"

The firstan town that they cam' till,
   He bought her brooch and ring;
But aye he bade her turn again,
   And nae farther gang wi' him.

" But again, dear love, and again, dear love,
   Will ye never love me again?
Alas! for loving you sae weel,
   And you nae me again!"

The second town that they cam' till,
   His heart it grew mair fain;
And he was as deep in love wi' her
   As she wi' him again.

The neistan town that they cam' till,
   He bought her wedding-gown ;
And made her lady o' ha's and bowers,
   In bonny Berwick town.

Anonymous.

A Love Sonnet

I LOVED a lass, a fair one,
   As fair as e'er was seen ;
She was indeed a rare on
   Another Sheba queen.
But fool as then I was,
   I thought she loved me too ;
But now, alas ! sh' 'as left me,
   Falero, lero, loo. . . . .

In summer time to Medley,
   My love and I would go ;
The boatmen then stood ready,
   My love and I to row.
For cream there would we call,
   For cake, and for prunes too ;
But now, alas ! sh' 'as left me,
   Falero, lero, loo. . . .

And as abroad we walked,
   As lovers' fashion is,
Oft as we sweetly talked
   The sun should steal a kiss.

The wind upon her lips
　　Likewise most sweetly blew ;
But now, alas ! sh' 'as left me,
　　Falero, lero, loo.

Her cheeks were like the cherry,
　　Her skin as white as snow ;
When she was blithe and merry,
　　She angel-like did show.
Her waist exceeding small,
　　The fives did fit her shoe ;
But now, alas ! sh' 'as left me,
　　Falero, lero, loo.

In summer time or winter
　　She had her heart's desire ;
I still did scorn to stint her
　　From sugar, sack, or fire.
The world went round about,
　　No cares we ever knew ;
But now, alas ! sh' 'as left me,
　　Falero, lero, loo. . . .

If ever that dame Nature,
　　For this false lover's sake,
Another pleasing creature
　　Like unto her should make
Let her remember this,
　　To make the other true ;
For this, alas ! hath left me,
　　Falero, lero, loo

No riches now can raise me,
   No want make me despair;
No misery amaze me,
   Nor yet for want I care.
I have lost a world itself,
   My earthly heaven, adieu,
Since she, alas! hath left me,
   Falero, lero, loo.

George Wither.

A Noble Youth

SO cruel prison how could betide, alas,
   As proud Windsor? where I, in lust and joy,
With a King's son, my childish years did pass,
In greater feast than Priam's sons of Troy:
Where each sweet place returns a taste full sour.
The large green courts, where we were wont to hove,
With eyes cast up into the Maiden's tower,
And easy sighs, such as folk draw in love.
The stately seats, the ladies bright of hue.
The dances short, long tales of great delight;
With words and looks that tigers could but rue;
Where each of us did plead the other's right.
The palme-play, where, despoiled for the game,
With dazzled eyes oft we by gleams of love
Have miss'd the ball, and got the sight of our dame,
To bait her eyes, which kept the leads above.

The gravel'd ground, with sleeves tied on the helm,
On foaming horse, with swords and friendly hearts;
With chere, as though one should another whelm,
Where we have fought, and chased oft with darts.
With silver drops the mead yet spread for ruth,
In active games of nimbleness and strength,
Where we did strain, trained with swarms of youth,
Our tender limbs, that yet shot up in length.
The secret groves, which oft we made resound
Of pleasant plaint, and of our ladies' praise ;
Recording oft what grace each one had found,
What hope of speed, what dread of long delays.
The wild forest, the clothed holts with green ;
With reins availed, and swift y-breathed horse,
With cry of hounds, and merry blasts between,
Where we did chase the fearful hart of force.
The wide vales eke, that harbour'd us each night:
Wherewith, alas ! reviveth in my breast
The sweet accord : such sleeps as yet delight ;
The pleasant dreams, the quiet bed of rest ;
The secret thoughts, imparted with such trust ;
The wanton talk, the divers change of play ;
The friendship sworn, each promise kept so just,
Wherewith we past the winter night away.
And with this thought the blood forsakes the face ;
The tears berain my cheeks of deadly hue :
The which, as soon as sobbing sighs, alas !
Up-supped have, thus I my plaint renew ı
" O place of bliss ! renewer of my woes !
Give me account, where is my noble fere ?
Whom in thy walls thou dost each night enclose ;

To other lief; but unto me most dear."
Echo, alas! that doth my sorrow rue,
Returns thereto a hollow sound of plaint.
Thus I alone, where all my freedom grew,
In prison pine, with bondage and restraint:
And with remembrance of the greater grief,
To banish the less, I find my chief relief.

Earl of Surrey

The Pulley

WHEN God at first made Man,
    Having a glass of blessings standing by;
Let us (said He) pour on him all we can:
Let the world's riches, which dispersèd lie,
    Contract into a span.

    So strength first made a way;
Then beauty flow'd, then wisdom, honour, pleasure:
When almost all was out, God made a stay,
Perceiving that alone, of all his treasure,
    Rest in the bottom lay.

    For if I should (said He)
Bestow this jewel also on my creature,
He would adore my gifts instead of me,
And rest in Nature, not the God of Nature:
    So both should losers be.

    Yet let him keep the rest,
But keep them with repining restlessness:
Let him be rich and weary, that at least,
If goodness lead him not, yet weariness
    May toss him to my breast.
                            George Herbert

Absent in the Spring   ᄾ   ᄾ

FROM you have I been absent in the spring,
    When proud-pied April, dress'd in all his trim,
Hath put a spirit of youth in everything,
That heavy Saturn laugh'd and leap'd with him.
Yet nor the lays of birds, nor the sweet smell
Of different flowers in odour and in hue,
Could make me any summer's story tell,
Or from their proud lap pluck them where they
    grew;
Nor did I wonder at the Lily's white,
Nor praise the deep vermilion of the Rose;
They were but sweet, but figures of delight,
Drawn after you, you pattern of all those.
    Yet seem'd it Winter still, and, you away,
    As with your shadow I with these did play.
                            Shakespeare.

Song ~ ~ ~ ~

LOVE is the blossom where there blows
　Every thing that lives or grows :
Love doth make the Heav'ns to move,
And the sun doth burn in love :
Love the strong and weak doth yoke,
And makes the ivy climb the oak,
Under whose shadows lions wild,
Soften'd by love, grow tame and mild :
Love no med'cine can appease,
He burns the fishes in the seas :
Not all the skill his wounds can stench,
Not all the sea his fire can quench.
Love did make the bloody spear
Once a leavy coat to wear,
While in his leaves there shrouded lay
Sweet birds, for love that sing and play.
And of all love's joyful flame
I the bud and blossom am.
　　Only bend thy knee to me,
　　Thy wooing shall thy winning be !

See, see the flowers that below
Now as fresh as morning blow ;
And of all the virgin rose
That as bright Aurora shows ;
How they all unleavèd die,
Losing their virginity !
Like unto a summer shade,
But now born, and now they fade.

Every thing doth pass away;
There is danger in delay:
Come, come, gather then the rose,
Gather it, or it you lose!
All the sand of Tagus' shore
Into my bosom casts his ore:
All the valleys' swimming corn
To my house is yearly borne:
Every grape of every vine
Is gladly bruised to make me wine:
While ten thousand kings as proud,
To carry up my train have bow'd,
And a world of ladies send me
In my chambers to attend me:
All the stars in Heav'n that shine,
And ten thousand more, are mine:
  Only bend thy knee to me,
  Thy wooing shall thy winning be!
Giles Fletcher.

The Ballad of Dowsabell

FAR in the country of Arden
 There wonn'd a knight, hight Cassamen,
  As bold as Isenbras;
Fell was he and eager bent
In battle and in tournament
  As was the good Sir Topas.

He had, as antique stories tell,
A daughter cleped Dowsabell,
  A maiden fair and free:

And for she was her father's heir,
Full well she was ycond the leir
    Of mickle courtesy.

The silk well could she twist and twine,
And make the fine March-pine,
    And with the needle work;
And she could help the priest to say
His Matins on a holy-day,
    And sing a psalm in kirk.

She wore a frock of frolic green
Might well become a maiden Queen,
    Which seemly was to see:
A hood to that so neat and fine,
In colour like the columbine
    Y-wrought full featously.

Her features all as fresh above
As is the grass that grows by Dove,
    And lithe as lass of Kent:
Her skin as soft as Lemster wool,
As white as snow on Peakish Hull,
    Or swan that swims in Trent.

This maiden, in a morn betime
Went forth when May was in her prime
    To get sweet setywall,
The honeysuckle, the harlock,
The lily and the lady-smock,
    To deck her summer hall.

Thus as she wander'd here and there
And picked of the bloomy brier,
    She chanced to espy
A shepherd sitting on a bank,
Like chanticleer he crowed crank,
    And pip'd full merrily.

He learn'd his sheep, as he him list,
When he would whistle in his fist
    To feed about him round.
Whilst he full many a carrol sang
Until the fields and meadows rang
    And all the woods did sound.

In favour this same shepherd swain
Was like the bedlam Tamerlane
    Which held proud kings in awe;
But meek as any lamb might be,
And innocent of ill as he
    Whom his lewd brother slaw.

The shepherd wore a sheep-gray cloak
Which was of the finest lock
    That could be cut with shear.
His mittens were of bauzon's skin,
His cockers were of cordiwin,
    His hood of miniveer.

His aule and lingel in a thong,
His tar-box on his broad belt hung,
    His breech of Cointree blue.

Full crisp and curled were his locks,
His brows as white as Albion rocks,
    So like a lover true.

And piping still he spent the day,
So merry as a popinjay,
    Which liked Dowsabell;
That would she ought, or would she nought,
This lad would never from her thought,
    She in love-longing fell.

At length she tucked up her frock,
White as a lily was her smock,
    She drew the shepherd nigh:
But then the shepherd pip'd a-good,
That all his sheep forsook their food,
    To hear his melody.

"Thy sheep," quoth she, "cannot be lean
That have a jolly shepherd swain
    The which can pipe so well";
"Yea, but," saith he, "their shepherd may,
If piping thus he pine away
    In love of Dowsabell."

"Of love, fond boy, take thou no keep,"
Quoth she, "look well unto thy sheep,
    Lest they should hap to stray."
Quoth he, "So had I done full well,
Had I not seen fair Dowsabell
    Come forth to gather May."

With that she 'gan to vail her head,
Her cheeks were like the roses red,
    But not a word she said ;
With that the shepherd 'gan to frown,
He threw his pretty pipes a-down
    And on the ground him laid.

Saith she, " I may not stay till night
And leave my summer hall undight,
    And all for love of thee."
" My cote," saith he, " nor yet my fold
Shall neither sheep nor shepherd hold
    Except thou favour me."

Saith she, " Yet liever I were dead,
Than I should lose my maiden head,
    And all for love of men."
Saith he, " Yet are you too unkind
If in your heart you cannot find
    To love us now and then :

" And I to thee will be as kind
As Colin was to Rosalind,
    Of courtesy the flower."
"Then I will be as true," quoth she
As ever maiden yet might be
    Unto her paramour : "

With that she bent her snow-white knee,
Down by the shepherd kneeled she
    And him she sweetly kist :

With that the shepherd whoop'd for joy,
Quoth he, "There's never shepherd's boy
    That ever was so blest."

Michael Drayton

The Lament of the Border Widow

MY love he built me a bonny bower,
    And clad it a' wi' lily flower;
A brawer bower ye ne'er did see
Than my true love he built for me.

There came a man, by middle day,
He spied his sport, and went away;
And brought the King that very night,
Who brake my bower and slew my knight.

He slew my knight, to me sae dear;
He slew my knight, and poin'd his gear;
My servants all for life did flee,
And left me in extremetie.

I sew'd his sheet, making my mane;
I watch'd the corpse, myself alane;
I watch'd his body night and day;
No living creature came that way.

I took his body on my back,
And whiles I gaed, and whiles I sat;
I digg'd a grave, and laid him in,
And happ'd him wi' the sod sae green.

But think na ye my heart was sair,
When I laid the moul' on his yellow hair?
O think na ye my heart was wae,
When I turn'd about, awa' to gae?

Nae living man I'll love again,
Since that my lovely knight is slain;
Wi' ae lock of his yellow hair
I'll chain my heart for evermair.
Anonymous.

Rosalind Muses ~ ~ ~

LOVE in my bosom like a bee
 Doth suck his sweet;
Now with his wings he plays with me,
 Now with his feet.
Within my eyes he makes his nest,
His bed amidst my tender breast;
My kisses are his daily feast,
And yet he robs me of my rest.
 Ah, wanton, will ye?

And if I sleep, then percheth he
 With pretty flight,
And makes his pillow of my knee
 The livelong night.
Strike I my lute, he tunes the string;
He music plays if so I sing;
He lends me every lovely thing;
Yet cruel he my heart doth sting.
 Whist, wanton, still ye!

Else I with roses every day
    Will whip you hence,
And bind you, when you long to play,
    For your offence.
I'll shut mine eyes to keep you in,
I'll make you fast it for your sin,
I'll count your power not worth a pin.
Alas, what hereby shall I win,
    If he gainsay me?

What if I beat the wanton boy
    With many a rod?
He will repay me with annoy,
    Because a god.
Then sit thou safely on my knee,
Then let thy bower my bosom be;
Lurk in mine eyes, I like of thee.
O Cupid, so thou pity me,
    Spare not, but play thee!

Thomas Lodge.

Song

FOR her gait, if she be walking;
    Be she sitting, I desire her
For her state's sake; and admire her
For her wit if she be talking;
    Gait and state and wit approve her;
    For which all and each I love her.

Be she sullen, I commend her
For a modest.   Be she merry,
For a kind one her prefer I.
Briefly, everything doth lend her
    So much grace, and so approve her,
    That for everything I love her.

William Browne.

Sarrazine's Song of
Pharamond's Grave

HATH any loved you well, down there,
    Summer or winter through?
Down there, have you found any fair
    Laid in the grave with you?
Is death's long kiss a richer kiss
    Than mine was wont to be—
Or have you gone to some far bliss
    And quite forgotten me?

What soft enamouring of sleep
    Hath you in some soft way?
What charmed death holdeth you with deep
    Strange lure by night and day?--
A little space below the grass,
    Out of the sun and shade;
But worlds away from me, alas,
    Down there where you are laid?

My bright hair's waved and wasted gold,
   What is it now to thee—
Whether the rose-red life I hold
   Or white death holdeth me?
Down there you love the grave's own green.
   And evermore you rave
Of some sweet seraph you have seen
   Or dreamt of in the grave.

There you shall lie as you have lain,
   Though in the world above
Another live your life again,
   Loving again your love:
Is it not sweet beneath the palm?
   Is not the warm day rife
With some long mystic golden calm
   Better than love and life?

The broad quaint odorous leaves like hands
   Weaving the fair day through,
Weave sleep no burnished bird withstands,
   While death weaves sleep for you;
And many a strange rich breathing sound
   Ravishes morn and noon:
And in that place you must have found
   Death a delicious swoon.

Hold me no longer for a word
   I used to say or sing:
Ah, long ago you must have heard
   So many a sweeter thing:

For rich earth must have reached your heart
   And turned the faith to flowers ;
And warm wind stolen, part by part,
   Your soul through faithless hours.

And many a soft seed must have won
   Soil of some yielding thought,
To bring a bloom up to the sun
   That else had ne'er been brought ;
And, doubtless, many a passionate hue
   Hath made that place more fair,
Making some passionate part of you
   Faithless to me down there.

Arthur W. E. O'Shaughnessy.

In the Orchard

LEAVE go my hands, let me catch breath and see ;
Let the dew-fall drench either side of me ;
   Clear apple-leaves are soft upon that moon
Seen sidelong like a blossom in the tree ;
   Ah God, ah God, that day should be so soon.

The grass is thick and cool, it lets us lie.
Kissed upon either cheek and either eye,
   I turn to thee as some green afternoon
Turns toward sunset, and is loth to die ;
   Ah God, ah God, that day should be so soon.

Lie closer, lean your face upon my side,
Feel where the dew fell that has hardly dried,
   Hear how the blood beats that went nigh to swoon;
The pleasure lives there when the sense has died;
   Ah God, ah God, that day should be so soon.

O my fair lord, I charge you leave me this:
Is it not sweeter than a foolish kiss?
   Nay take it then, my flower, my first in June,
My rose, so like a tender mouth it is:
   Ah God, ah God, that day should be so soon.

Love, till dawn sunder night from day with fire,
Dividing my delight and my desire,
   The crescent life and love the plenilune,
Love me though dusk begin and dark retire;
   Ah God, ah God, that day should be so soon.

Ah, my heart fails, my blood draws back; I know,
When life runs over, life is near to go;
   And with the slain of love love's ways are strewn,
And with their blood, if love will have it so;
   Ah God, ah God, that day should be so soon.

Ah, do thy will now; slay me if thou wilt;
There is no building now the walls are built,
   No quarrying now the corner-stone is hewn,
No drinking now the vine's whole blood is spilt;
   Ah God, ah God, that day should be so soon.

Nay, slay me now; nay, for I will be slain;
Pluck thy red pleasure from the teeth of pain,
   Break down thy vine ere yet grape-gatherers prune,
Slay me ere day can slay desire again;
   Ah God, ah God, that day should be so soon.

Yea, with thy sweet lips, with thy sweet sword; yea,
Take life and all, for I will die, I say;
   Love, I gave love, is life a better boon?
For sweet night's sake I will not live till day;
   Ah God, ah God, that day should be so soon.

Nay, I will sleep then only; nay, but go.
Ah sweet, too sweet to me, my sweet, I know
   Love, sleep, and death go to the sweet same tune;
Hold my hair fast, and kiss me through it so.
   Ah God, ah God, that day should be so soon.

                Algernon Charles Swinburne.

O Mistress Mine

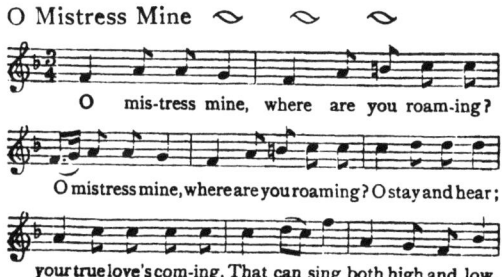

O mistress mine, where are you roaming? O stay and hear;
your true love's coming, That can sing both high and low.

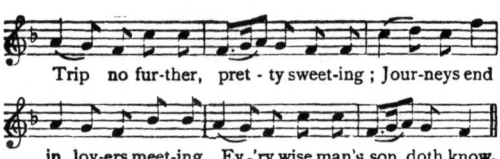

II

What is love? 'Tis not hereafter;
Present mirth hath present laughter;
  What's to come is still unsure:
In delay there lies no plenty;
Then come kiss me, Sweet-and-twenty,
  Youth's a stuff will not endure.

William Shakespeare.

Love will find out the Way

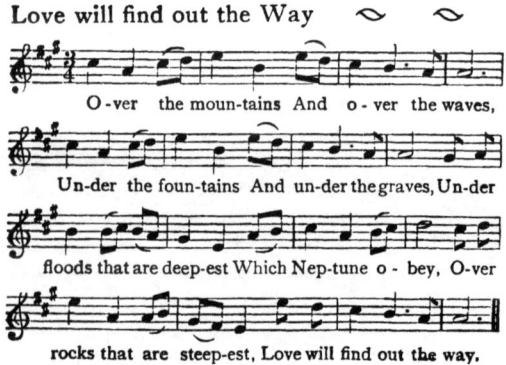

II

Where there is no place
  For the glow-worm to lie,
Where there is no space
  For receipt of a fly,
Where the midge dares not venture
  Lest herself fast she lay,
If Love come he will enter
  And soon find out his way.

III

You may esteem him
  A child for his might,
Or you may deem him
  A coward from his flight;
But if she whom Love doth honour
  Be concealed from the day,
Set a thousand guards upon her,
  Love will find out the way.

IV

Some think to lose him
  By having him confined,
And some do suppose him,
  Poor thing, to be blind;
But if ne'er so close ye wall him,
  Do the best that you may,
Blind Love, if so ye call him,
  Soon will find out his way.

V

You may train the eagle
  To stoop to your fist,

Or you may inveigle
   The Phœnix of the east;
The lioness, you may move her
   To give over her prey;
But you'll ne'er stop a lover,
   He will find out his way.

Anonymous.

II

Her father he makes cabbage-nets
   And in the streets does cry 'em,
Her mother she sells laces long
   To such as please to buy 'em ;
But sure such folks could ne'er beget
   So sweet a girl as Sally;
She is the darling of my heart,
   And she lives in our alley.

III

When she is by I leave my work,
   I love her so sincerely,
My master comes like any Turk
   And bangs me most severely ;
But let him bang his belly full,
   I'll bear it all for Sally;
She is the darling of my heart,
   And she lives in our alley.

IV

Of all the days that's in the week
   I dearly love but one day,
And that's the day that comes betwixt
   A Saturday and Monday ;
For then I'm dressed all in my best
   To walk abroad with Sally :
She is the darling of my heart,
   And she lives in our alley.

V

My master carries me to church,
    And often am I blamed
Because I leave him in the lurch
    As soon as text is named;
I leave the church in sermon-time
    And slink away to Sally;
She is the darling of my heart,
    And she lives in our alley.

VI

When Christmas comes about again
    O then I shall have money,
I'll hoard it up and box it all,
    And give it to my honey;
I would it were ten thousand pound,
    I'd give it all to Sally;
She is the darling of my heart,
    And she lives in our alley.

VII

My master and the neighbours all
    Make game of me and Sally,
And, but for her, I'd better be
    A slave and row a galley;
But when my seven long years are out
    O then I'll marry Sally—
O then we'll wed and then we'll bed . . .
    But not in our alley!

The Message

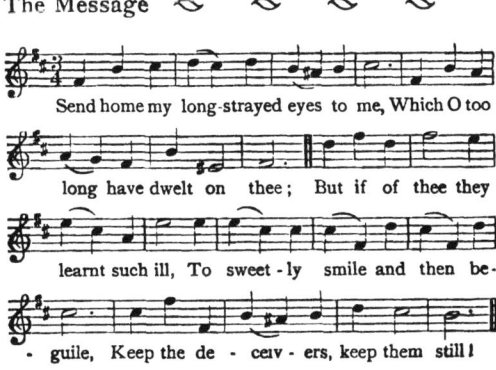

Send home my long-strayed eyes to me, Which O too long have dwelt on thee; But if of thee they learnt such ill, To sweet-ly smile and then be-guile, Keep the de-ceiv-ers, keep them still!

II

Send home my harmless Heart again,
Which no unworthy thought could stain:
But if it has been taught by thine
To forfeit both its word and oath,
Keep it; for then 'tis none of mine!

III

Yet send me home my heart and eyes,
That I may see, and know thy Lies!
That I one day may Laugh, when thou
Shall grieve for one, thy Love will scorn,
And prove as false as thou art now!

After John Donne.

The Seamew

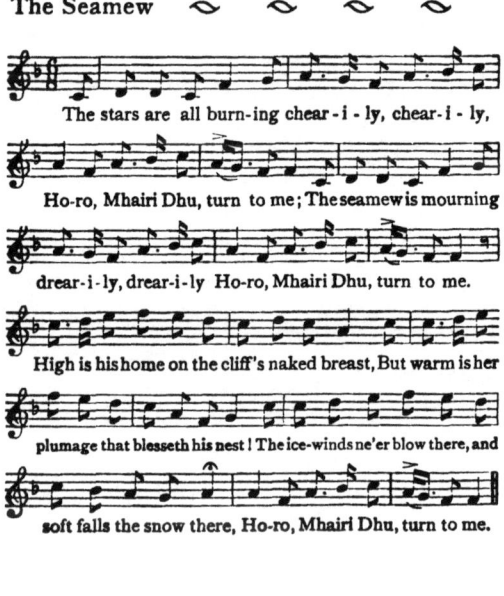

The stars are all burning chear-i-ly, chear-i-ly, Ho-ro, Mhairi Dhu, turn to me; The seamew is mourning drear-i-ly, drear-i-ly Ho-ro, Mhairi Dhu, turn to me.

High is his home on the cliff's naked breast, But warm is her plumage that blesseth his nest! The ice-winds ne'er blow there, and soft falls the snow there, Ho-ro, Mhairi Dhu, turn to me.

Blow, Blow, thou Winter Wind

Blow, blow, thou win-ter wind, Thou art not so un-kind, Thou art not so un-kind as man's in-gra-ti-

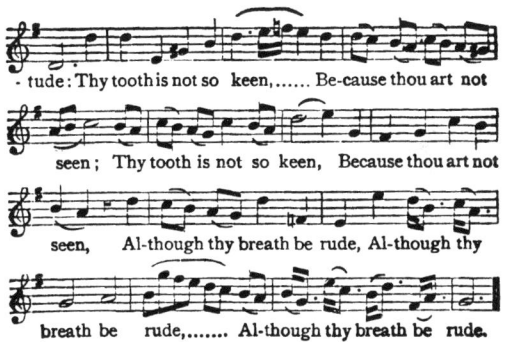

- tude: Thy tooth is not so keen,...... Be-cause thou art not seen; Thy tooth is not so keen, Because thou art not seen, Al-though thy breath be rude, Al-though thy breath be rude,....... Al-though thy breath be rude.

II

Freeze, freeze, thou bitter sky,
Thou dost not bite so nigh
As benefits forgot:
Though thou the waters warp,
Thy sting is not so sharp
As friend remembered not.

William Shakespeare.

All round my Hat

From "A Garland of Country Song" (Methuen)

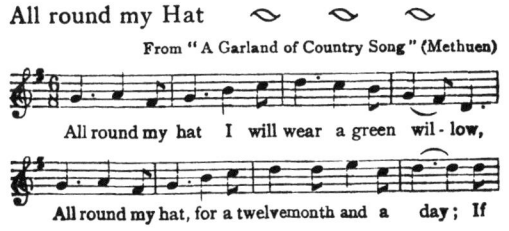

All round my hat I will wear a green wil-low, All round my hat, for a twelvemonth and a day; If

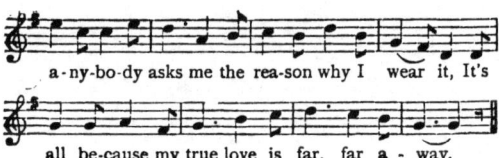

a-ny-bo-dy asks me the rea-son why I wear it, It's all be-cause my true love is far, far a-way.

II

My love she was fair, and my love she was kind, too,
    And many were the happy hours between my love and me;
I never could refuse her whatever she'd a mind to,
    But now she's far away, far across the stormy sea.

III

O will my love be true, and will my love be faithful?
    Or will she find another swain to court her where she's gone?
The men will all run after her, so pretty and so graceful,
    And perhaps she may forget me, lamenting all alone.

IV

So all round my hat I will wear a green willow,
    All round my hat for a twelvemonth and a day;
If anybody asks me the reason why I wear it,
    It's all because my true love is far, far away.

O what if the Fowler

Old Manx air. By permission of W. H. Gill and Boosey & Co

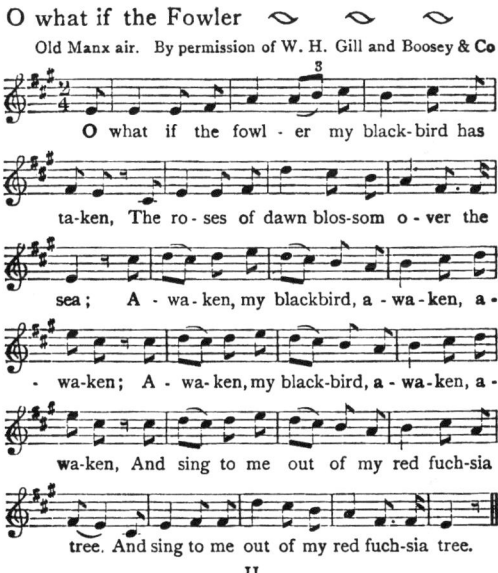

O what if the fowl-er my black-bird has ta-ken, The ro-ses of dawn blos-som o-ver the sea; A-wa-ken, my blackbird, a-wa-ken, a-wa-ken; A-wa-ken, my black-bird, a-wa-ken, a-wa-ken, And sing to me out of my red fuch-sia tree. And sing to me out of my red fuch-sia tree.

II

O what if the fowler my blackbird has taken?
  The sun lifts his head from the lap of the sea —
Awaken, my blackbird, awaken, awaken,
  And sing to me out of my red fuchsia tree!

III

O what if the fowler my blackbird has taken?
  The mountain grows white with the birds of the sea;
But down in my garden forsaken, forsaken,
  I'll weep all the day by my red fuchsia tree!

Charles Dalmon.

Now, O Now

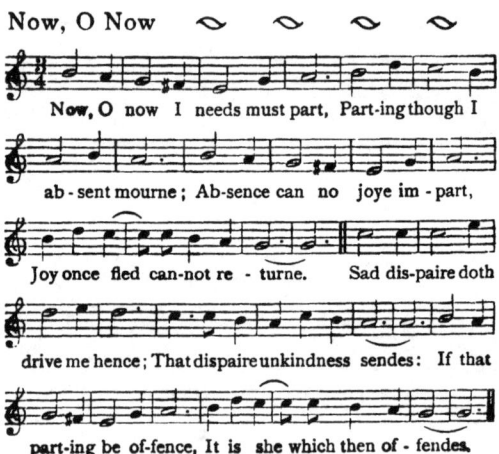

Now, O now I needs must part, Part-ing though I ab-sent mourne; Ab-sence can no joye im-part, Joy once fled can-not re - turne. Sad dis-paire doth drive me hence; That dispaire unkindness sendes: If that part-ing be of-fence, It is she which then of - fendes.

II

Deare, when I from thee am gone,
Gone are all my joies at once;
I loved thee and thee alone,
In whose love I joyed once.
And although your sight I leave,
Sight wherein my joies doe lie,
Till that death doe sense bereave
Never shall affection die.

III

Deare, if I doe not returne
Love and I shall die together;
For my absence never mourne
Whom you might have joyed ever.

Part we must though now I die,
Die I doe to part with you;
Him dispaire doth cause to lie
Who both lived and dieth true.

Like as the Lark

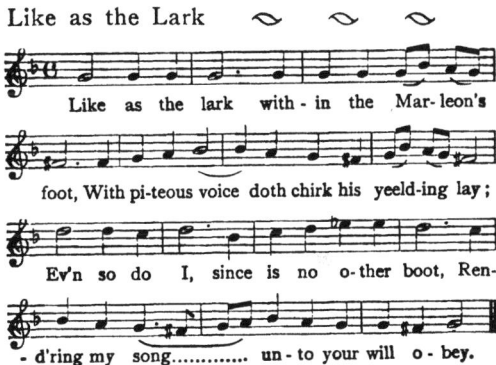

Like as the lark with-in the Mar-leon's foot, With pi-teous voice doth chirk his yeeld-ing lay; Ev'n so do I, since is no o-ther boot, Ren-d'ring my song............ un-to your will o-bey.

II

Your vertue mounts above my force so high,
That with your beauties seared I am so sure,
That there remains resistance none in me;
But patiently your pleasure to endure.

III

And in your will my fancie shall depend,
My life and death consists into your will,
I rather would my life were at an end,
Than in despair this way continue still.

IV

And since there is no pity more in place,
But that your cruelty doth thrist my blood,
I am content to have no other grace,
But let it out, if it may do you good.

La Fille du Roy

II

Las! Il n'a nul mal qui n'a le mal d'amour!
Le bon roy lui dit: Ma fille, qu' avez-vous?
Voulez-vous un mari?—Hélas, oui, mon seignoux!
Las! Il n'a nul mal qui n'a le mal d'amour!

Amarillys

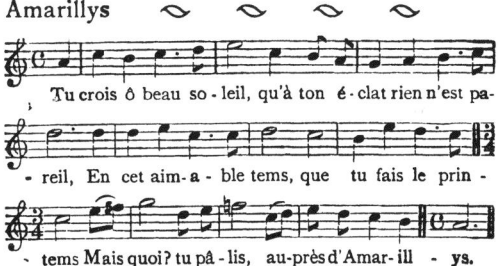

Tu crois ô beau soleil, qu'à ton éclat rien n'est pareil, En cet aimable tems, que tu fais le printems Mais quoi? tu pâlis, auprès d'Amarillys.

II

Or que le ciel est gai,
Durant ce gentil mois de mai,
Les roses vont fleurir,
Les lys s'épanouir :
Mais que sont les lys
Auprès d'Amarillys ?

III

De ses nouvelles pleurs
L'aube va ranimer les fleurs ;
Mais que fait leur beauté
A mon cœur attristé,
Quand des pleurs je lis
Aux yeux d'Amarillys ?

Louis XIII, *King of France.*

The Bailiff's Daughter of Islington

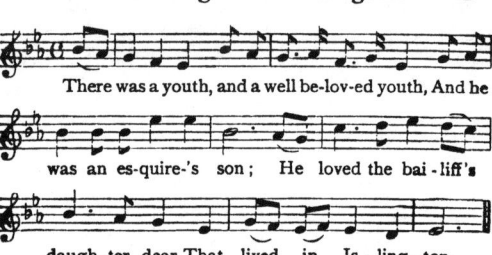

There was a youth, and a well be-lov-ed youth, And he was an es-quire-'s son; He loved the bai-liff's daugh-ter dear That lived in Is-ling-ton.

II

She was coy, and she would not believe
  That he did love her so,
No, nor at any time she would
  Any countenance to him show

III

But when his friends did understand
  His fond and foolish mind,
They sent him up to fair London,
  An apprentice for to bind.

IV

And when he had been seven long years,
  And his love he had not seen,
"Many a tear have I shed for her sake
  When she little thought of me."

V

All the maids of Islington
  Went forth to sport and play,
All but the bailiff's daughter,—
  She secretly stole away.

VI

She put off her gown of gray,
  And put on her puggish attire.
She's up to fair London gone
  Her true love to require.

VII

As she went along the road,
  The weather being hot and dry,
There was she aware of her true-love,
  At length came riding by.

VIII

She stepped to him, as red as any rose,
  And took him by the bridle ring:
"I pray you, kind sir, give me one penny,
  To ease my weary limb."

IX

"I prithee, sweet heart, canst thou tell me
  Where that thou wast born?"
"At Islington, kind sir," said she,
  "Where I have had many a scorn."

X

"I prithee, sweet heart, canst thou tell me
  Whether thou dost know
The bailiff's daughter of Islington?"
  "She's dead, sir, long ago."

XI

"Then will I sell my goodly steed,
  My saddle and my bow;
I will unto some far countree
  Where no man doth me know."

XII

"O stay, O stay! thou goodly youth,
  She's alive, she is not dead;
Here she standeth by thy side,
  And is ready to be thy bride."

XIII

"O farewell grief! and welcome joy!
  Ten thousand times and more,
For now I have seen my own true love
  That I thought I should have seen no more."

Rio Grande

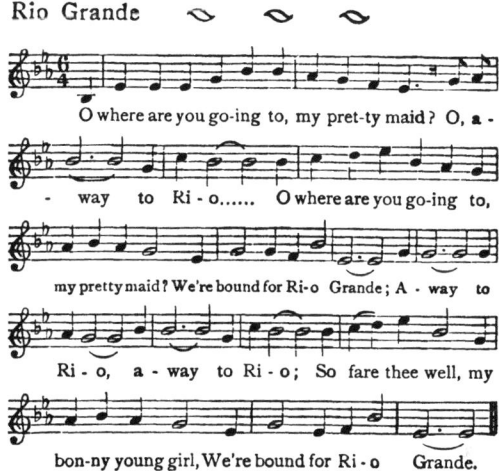

II

O have you a sweetheart, my pretty maid?
    O away to Rio ;
O have you a sweetheart, my pretty maid?
    We're bound for Rio Grande.

Away to Rio, away to Rio,
So fare thee well, my bonny young girl,
We're bound for Rio Grande.

VILLAGE AND INN

Clare's Desire

BESIDE a runnel build my shed,
   With stubbles cover'd o'er ;
Let broad oaks o'er its chimney spread,
   And grass-plats grace the door.

The door may open with a string,
   So that it closes tight :
And locks would be a wanted thing,
   To keep out thieves at night.

A little garden, not too fine,
   Inclose with painted pales ;
And woodbines, round the cot to twine,
   Pin to the walls with nails.

Let hazels grow, and spindling sedge,
   Bent bowering overhead ;
Dig old man's beard from woodland hedge,
   To twine a summer shade.

Beside the threshold sods provide,
   And build a summer seat ;
Plant sweet-briar bushes by its side,
   And flowers that blossom sweet.

I love the sparrows' ways to watch
   Upon the cotters' sheds,
So here and there pull out the thatch,
   That they may hide their heads.

And as the sweeping swallows stop
   Their flights along the green,
Leave holes within the chimney-top
   To paste their nest between.

Stick shelves and cupboards round the hut,
   In all the holes and nooks ;
Nor in the cottage fail to put
   A cupboard for the books.

Along the floor some sand I'll sift,
   To make it fit to live in ;
And then I'll thank ye for the gift,
   As something worth the giving.
                                        John Clare.

From "The Garden"   ᙥ   ᙥ   ᙥ

OH blessed shades ! oh gentle cool retreat
   From all th' immoderate Heat,
In which the frantick world does burn and sweat !
This does the Lion Star, Ambitions rage ;
This Avarice, the Dog Star's Thirst asswage ;
Every where else their fatal power we see,
They make and rule Man's wretched Destinie :
   They neither set, nor disappear,
   But tyrannize o'er all the year ;
Whilst we ne'er feel their Flame nor Influence here
   The birds that dance from bough to bough,
   And sing above in every Tree,
   Are not from Fears and Cares more free,

Than we who Lie or Walk below,
   And should by right be Singers too.
What Prince's Quire of Musick can excel
   That which within this shade does dwell?
   To which we nothing Pay or Give,
   They like all other Poets live,
Without reward, or thanks for their obliging pains;
   'Tis well if they become not Prey:
The whistling winds add their less artful strains,
And a grave Base the murmuring fountains play:
Nature does all this Harmony bestow,
   But to our Plants, Art's Musick too,
The Pipe, Theorbo, and Guitar we owe;
The Lute itself, which once was Green and Mute,
   When *Orpheus* struck th' inspired Lute,
   The Trees danc'd round, and understood
   By Sympathy, the voice of wood.

Abraham Cowley.

From "Appleton House"

HOW safe, methinks, and strong, behind
   These trees, have I incamped my mind;
Where beauty, aiming at the heart,
Bends in some tree its useless dart,
And where the world no certain shot
Can make, or me it toucheth not,
But I on it securely play,
And gall its horsemen all the day.

Bind me, ye woodbines, in your twines;
Curl me about, ye gadding vines;
And oh, so close your circles lace,
That I may never leave this place!
But, lest your fetters prove too weak,
Ere I your silken bondage break,
Do you, O brambles, chain me too,
And, courteous briars, nail me through!

Andrew Marvell.

The Wish

IF I live to be Old, for I find I go down,
   Let this be my Fate. In a Country Town,
May I have a warm House, with a Stone at the Gate,
And a cleanly young Girl, to rub my bald Pate.

Chorus.

May I govern my Passion with an absolute Sway,
And grow Wiser, and Better, as my Strength wears away,
Without Gout, or Stone, by a gentle decay.

May my little House stand on the Side of a Hill,
With an easy Descent, to a Mead, and a Mill,
That when I've a mind, I may hear my Boy read,
In the Mill, if it rains, if it's dry, in the Mead.

Near a shady Grove, and a murmuring Brook,
With the Ocean at Distance, whereupon I may look,
With a spacious Plain, without Hedge or Stile,
And an easy Pad-Nag, to ride out a Mile.

With *Horace* and *Petrarch*, and Two or Three more
Of the best Wits that reign'd in the Ages before,
With roast Mutton, rather than Ven'son or Teal,
And clean, tho' coarse Linnen at every Meal.

With a Pudding on Sundays, with stout humming liquor,
And Remnants of Latin to welcome the Vicar,
With *Monte-fiascone* or *Burgundy* Wine,
To drink the King's Health as oft as I dine.

Tho' I care not for Riches, may I not be so poor,
That the Rich without shame cannot enter my Door,
May they court my converse, may they take much delight,
My old Stories to hear in a Winter's long Night.

May none whom I love, to so great Riches rise
As to slight their Acquaintance, and their old Friends despise.
So low, or so high, may none of them be,
As to move either Pity, or Envy in me.

I hope I shall have no occasion to send
For Priests, or Fysicians, till I am so near mine End
That I have eat all my Bread and drunk my last Glass,
Let them come then, and set their Seals to my Pass.

With a Courage undaunted, may I face my last Day,
And when I am dead may the better sort say,
In the Morning, when sober, in the Evening, when mellow,
He's gone, and left not behind him his Fellow.
            Walter Pope.

I Got Two Fields ∽   ∽   ∽   ∽

I GOT two viel's, an' I don't kiare
  What squire mid have a bigger shiare.
My little zummer-leäse da stratch
Al doun the hangen, to a patch
O' meäd between a hedge an' rank
Ov elems, an' a river bank,
Wher yoller clotes in spreaden beds
O' floaten leaves da lift ther heads
By benden bullrushes an' zedge
A-swâyen at the water's edge,
Below the withy that da spread
Athirt the brook his wold grey head,

An' eltrot flowers, milky white,
Da catch the slanten evemen light;
An' in the miaple boughs, along
The hedge, da ring the blackbird's zong;
Or in the dae, a-vleeren droo
The leafy trees, the huosse gookoo
Da zing to mowers that da zet
Their zives on end, an' stan' to whet.
From my wold house among the trees
A liane da goo along the leäse,
O' yoller gravel doun between
Two meshy banks var ever green.
An' trees, a-hangen auverhead,
Da hide a trinklen gully bed,
A-cover'd by a brudge var hoss
Or man a-voot to come across.
Zoo wi' my huomestead I don't kiare
What squire mid have a bigger shiare.

William Barnes.

From "The Castle of Indolence"

O MORTAL man, who livest here by toil,
    Do not complain of this thy hard estate;
That like an emmet thou must ever moil,
Is a sad sentence of an ancient date;
And, certes, there is for it reason great;
For, though sometimes it makes thee weep and wail,
And curse thy star, and early drudge and late;

Withouten that would come an heavier bale,
Loose life, unruly passions, and diseases pale.

In lowly dale, fast by a river's side,
With woody hill o'er hill encompass'd round,
A most enchanting wizard did abide,
Than whom a fiend more fell is no where found.
It was, I ween, a lovely spot of ground;
And there a season atween June and May,
Half prankt with Spring, with summer half imbrown'd,
A listless climate made, where, sooth to say,
No living wight could work, ne cared even for play.

Was nought around but images of rest:
Sleep-soothing groves, and quiet lawns between;
And flowery beds that slumbrous influence kest,
From poppies breath'd; and beds of pleasant green,
Where never yet was creeping creature seen.
Meantime, unnumber'd glittering streamlets play'd,
And hurled every-where their waters sheen;
That, as they bicker'd through the sunny glade,
Though restless still themselves, a lulling murmur made.

Join'd to the prattle of the purling rills,
Were heard the lowing herds along the vale,
And flocks loud-bleating from the distant hills,
And vacant shepherds piping in the dale;
And, now and then, sweet Philomel would wail,

Or stock-doves plain amid the forest deep,
That drowsy rustled to the sighing gale;
And still a coil the grasshopper did keep;
Yet all these sounds yblent inclined all to sleep.

Full in the passage of the vale, above,
A sable, silent, solemn forest stood;
Where nought but shadowy forms was seen to move,
As Idless fancied in her dreaming mood:
And up the hills, on either side, a wood
Of blackening pines, aye waving to and fro,
Sent forth a sleepy horror through the blood;
And where this valley winded out, below,
The murmuring main was heard, and scarcely heard, to flow.

A pleasing land of drowsy-head it was,
Of dreams that wave before the half-shut eye;
And of gay castles in the clouds that pass,
For ever flushing round a summer-sky:
There eke the soft delights, that witchingly
Instil a wanton sweetness through the breast,
And the calm pleasures always hover'd nigh;
But whate'er smack'd of noyance, or unrest,
Was far, far off expell'd from this delicious rest.

James Thomson.

The Sunflower

AH Sunflower, weary of time,
   Who countest the steps of the Sun;
Seeking after that sweet golden clime
   Where the traveller's journey is done;

Where the Youth pined away with desire,
   And the pale Virgin shrouded in snow,
Arise from their graves, and aspire
   Where my Sunflower wishes to go!

William Blake.

To Penshurst

THOU art not, Penshurst, built to envious show,
   Of touch, or marble; nor canst boast a row
Of polish'd pillars, or a roof of gold:
Thou hast no lantern, whereof tales are told;
Or stair, or courts; but stand'st an ancient pile,
And these grudg'd at, art reverenced the while.
Thou joy'st in better marks, of soil, of air,
Of wood, of water; therein thou art fair.
Thou hast thy walks for health, as well as sport;
Thy mount, to which the Dryads do resort,
Where Pan and Bacchus their high feasts have
   made,
Beneath the broad beech, and the chestnut shade;
That taller tree, which of a nut was set,
At his great birth, where all the Muses met.
There, in the writhed bark, are cut the names
Of many a Sylvan, taken with his flames;

And thence the ruddy Satyrs oft provoke
The lighter Fauns, to reach thy Lady's oak.
Thy copse, too, named of Gamage, thou hast there,
That never fails to serve thee season'd deer,
When thou wouldst feast or exercise thy friends.
The lower land, that to the river bends,
Thy sheep, thy bullocks, kine, and calves do feed;
The middle grounds thy mares, and horses breed.
Each bank doth yield thee conies; and the tops
Fertile of wood, Ashore and Sidney's copps,
To crown thy open table, doth provide
The purpled pheasant, with the speckled side:
The painted partridge lies in ev'ry field,
And for thy mess is willing to be kill'd.
And if the high-swoln Medway fail thy dish,
Thou hast thy ponds, that pay thee tribute fish,
Fat aged carps that run into thy net,
And pikes, now weary their own kind to eat,
As loth the second draught or cast to stay,
Officiously at first themselves betray.
Bright eels that emulate them, and leap on land,
Before the fisher, or into his hand.
Then hath thy orchard fruit, thy garden flowers,
Fresh as the air, and new as are the hours.
The early cherry, with the later plum,
Fig, grape, and quince, each in his time doth come;
The blushing apricot, and woolly peach
Hang on thy walls, that every child may reach.
And though thy walls be of the country stone,
They're reared with no man's ruin, no man's groan;

There's none, that dwell about them, wish them down;
But all come in, the farmer and the clown;
And no one empty-handed, to salute
Thy lord and lady, though they have no suit.
Some bring a capon, some a rural cake,
Some nuts, some apples; some that think they make
The better cheeses, bring them; or else send
By their ripe daughters, whom they would commend
This way to husbands; and whose baskets bear
An emblem of themselves in plum, or pear.
But what can this (more than express their love)
Add to thy free provisions, far above
The need of such? whose liberal board doth flow,
With all that hospitality doth know!
Where comes no guest, but is allowed to eat,
Without his fear, and of thy lord's own meat:
Where the same beer and bread, and self-same wine,
That is his lordship's, shall be also mine:
And I not fain to sit (as some this day,
At great men's tables) and yet dine away.
Here no man tells my cups; nor standing by,
A waiter, doth my gluttony envy:
But gives me what I call for, and lets me eat,
He knows, below, he shall find plenty of meat;
Thy tables hoard not up for the next day,
Nor, when I take my lodging, need I pray
For fire, or lights, or livery; all is there;
As if thou then wert mine, or I reign'd here:

There's nothing I can wish, for which I stay.
That found King James, when hunting late, this
    way,
With his brave son, the prince, they saw thy fires
Shine bright on every hearth, as the desires
Of thy Penates had been set on flame,
To entertain them ; or the country came,
With all their zeal, to warm their welcome here.
What (great, I will not say, but) sudden chear
Didst thou then make 'em ! and what praise was
    heap'd
On thy good lady, then ! who therein reap'd
The just reward of her high huswifry ;
To have her linen, plate, and all things nigh,
When she was far ; and not a room, but drest,
As if it had expected such a guest !
These, Penshurst, are thy praise, and yet not all.
Thy lady's noble, fruitful, chaste withal.
His children thy great lord may call his own :
A fortune, in this age, but rarely known.
They are, and have been taught religion ; thence
Their gentler spirits have suck'd innocence.
Each morn, and even, they are taught to pray,
With the whole household, and may, every day,
Read in their virtuous parents' noble parts,
The mysteries of manners, arms, and arts.
Now, Penshurst, they that will proportion thee
With other edifices, when they see
Those proud ambitious heaps, and nothing else,
May say, their lords have built, but thy lord dwells.
                                        Ben Jonson.

Epitaph: Tewkesbury Abbey

Elianor Freeman

O VIRGIN blossome, in her May,
   Of Youth and Virtues, turn'd to clay,
Rich Earth! accomplisht with those graces
That adorne Saints for Heavenly places!
Let not Death boast his conquering powe',
Shee'le rise a Starre, that fell a flower.

Deceased May the 3d
An 1653, aged 21

Upon the Priory Grove, his usual retirement

HAIL, sacred shades! cool leafy house!
   Chaste treasurer of all my vows
And wealth! on whose soft bosom laid
My love's first steps I first betrayed:
Henceforth no melancholy flight,
No sad wing, or hoarse bird of Night,
Disturb this air, no fatal throat
Of raven, or owl, awake the note
Of our laid Echo, no voice dwell
Within these leaves but Philomel.
The poisonous ivy here no more
His false twists on the oak shall score;
Only the woodbine here may twine,
As th' emblem of her love, and mine;

The amorous sun shall here convey
His best beams, in thy shade to play;
The active air, the gentlest showers
Shall from his wings rain on thy flowers;
And the moon from her dewy locks,
Shall deck thee with her brightest drops:
Whatever can a fancy move,
Or feed the eye: be on this grove.

   And when, at last, the winds and tears
Of Heaven, with the consuming years,
Shall these green curls bring to decay,
And clothe thee in an agèd grey:—
If aught a lover can foresee:
Or if we poets prophets be—
From hence transplanted, thou shalt stand
A fresh grove in th' Elysian land;
Where—most blest pair!—as here on Earth
Thou first didst eye our growth, and birth;
So there again, thou'lt see us move
In our first innocence and love;
And in thy shades, as now, so then,
We'll kiss, and smile, and walk again.

                               Henry Vaughan.

A Sampler
Llanddeusaint, Caermarthenshire

PRESERVE me, Lord, amidst the crowd
   From every thought that's vain and proud,
And raise my wandering eyes to see
How good it is to trust in Thee.

The Belfry

DARK is the stair, and humid the old walls
    Wherein it winds, on worn stones, up the tower.
Only by loophole chinks at intervals
Pierces the late glow of this August hour.

Two truant children climb the stairway dark,
With joined hands, half in glee and half in fear,
The boy mounts brisk, the girl hangs back to hark
If the gruff sexton their light footsteps hear.

Dazzled at last they gain the belfry-room.
Barred rays through shutters hover across the floor
Dancing in dust; so fresh they come from gloom
That breathless they pause wondering at the door.

How hushed it is! what smell of timbers old
From cobwebbed beams! The warm light here and there
Edging a darkness, sleeps in pools of gold,
Or weaves fantastic shadows through the air.

How motionless the huge bell! Straight and stiff,
Ropes through the floor rise to the rafters dim.
The shadowy round of metal hangs, as if
No force could ever lift its gleamy rim.

A child's awe, a child's wonder, who shall trace
What dumb thoughts on its waxen softness write
In such a spell-brimmed, time-forgotten place,
Bright in that strangeness of approaching night?

As these two gaze, their fingers tighter press ;
For suddenly the slow bell upward heaves
Its vast mouth, the cords quiver at the stress,
And ere the heart prepare, the ear receives

Full on its delicate sense the plangent stroke
Of violent, iron, reverberating sound.
As if the tower in all its stones awoke,
Deep echoes tremble, again in clangour drowned,

That starts without a whir of frighted wings
And holds these young hearts shaken, hushed, and thrilled,
Like frail reeds in a rushing stream, like strings
Of music, or like trees with tempest filled,

And rolls in wide waves out o'er the lone land,
Tone following tone toward the far-setting sun,
Till where in fields long shadowed reapers stand
Bowed heads look up, and lo, the day is done.

At last it ebbs. Then silence on the last
Vibrating murmur builds its gradual weight ;
Another silence from that silence past,
Charged with the will of only sleeping Fate,

Such as some venturous listener appals
In world-old forest, when, untouched by hand,
Utterly ripe, a great tree crashing falls
And not a sound succeeds. The children stand

Rapt in that silence with the life-lit eye
Of expectation, and awe-parted lips;
Yet in their breasts the heart is beating high,
Flushed are they, tingling to the finger-tips

With a dim sense of the world's meaning changed,
And Time dissolved, and a lost freedom found
As if the soul had glimpse of regions ranged
Ere she was born into these senses bound.

They know not yet. But surely once again
Some touch of chance, a thought upon some face,
A sunned wall, a far voice, still midnight rain,
Shall strike them home into this hour and place.

And seized by memory in profounder spell,
So shall they listen with suspended breath
While, like that solemnly awakened bell,
Life deepens out to mystery more than Death;

And thrilling fear, like hope, to grandeur grown,
Losing the world, lets, ocean-vast, inroll
The power and glory of all that is unknown
Yet seeks in us the secret and the soul

Laurence Binyon.

Church-Musick ～　～　～　～

SWEETEST of sweets, I thank you: when displeasure
  Did through my bodie wound my minde,
You took me thence, and in your house of pleasure
  A daintie lodging me assign'd.

Now I in you without a bodie move,
  Rising and falling with your wings :
We both together sweetly live and love,
  Yet say sometimes, *God help poore Kings.*

Comfort, 'Ile die ; for if you poste from me,
  Sure I shall do so, and much more :
But if I travell in your companie,
  You know the way to heavens doore.

George Herbert.

The Little Vagabond

DEAR mother, dear mother, the Church is cold;
  But the Alehouse is healthy, and pleasant, and warm.
Besides, I can tell where I am used well ;
The poor parsons with wind like a blown bladder swell.

But, if at the Church they would give us some ale,
And a pleasant fire our souls to regale,
We'd sing and we'd pray all the livelong day,
Nor ever once wish from the Church to stray.

Then the Parson might preach, and drink, and sing,
And we'd be as happy as birds in the spring ;
And modest Dame Lurch, who is always at church,
Would not have bandy children, nor fasting, nor birch.

And God, like a father, rejoicing to see
His children as pleasant and happy as he,
Would have no more quarrel with the Devil or the barrel,
But kiss him, and give him both drink and apparel.

William Blake.

Epitaph on an Innkeeper

ONE butt sufficed a royal Duke to drown :
    Thee not a hundred butts, good old John Brown !

A Tavern Rhyme

"The Plough" at Ford in the Cotswolds

YE weary travelers that pass by,
    With dust and scorching sunbeams dry,
Or be ye numb'd with snow and frost
With having these bleak Cotswolds crost,
Step in and quaff my nut-brown ale,
Bright as rubys, mild and stale,
'Twill make your laging trotters dance
As nimble as the suns of France,
Then ye will owne, ye men of sense,
That neare was better spent six pence.

Epitaph in a Cornish Churchyard

OUR life is but a summer's day.
   Some only breakfast and away:
Others to dinner stay and are full fed:
The oldest only sups and goes to bed.
Long is his score who lingers out the day,
Who goes the soonest has the least to pay.

Lubber Breeze

THE four sails of the mill
   Like stocks stand still;
Their lantern-length is white
On blue more bright.

Unruffled is the mead,
Where lambkins feed
And sheep and cattle browse
And donkeys drowse.

Never the least breeze will
The wet thumb chill
That the anxious miller lifts,
Till the vane shifts.

The breeze in the great flour-bin
Is snug tucked in;
The lubber, while rats thieve,
Laughs in his sleeve.

T. Sturge Moore.

Mariana

WITH blackest moss the flower-plots
　　Were thickly crusted, one and all:
The rusted nails fall from the knots
　　That held the peach to the garden-wall.
The broken sheds look'd sad and strange:
　　Unlifted was the clinking latch;
　　Weeded and worn the ancient thatch
Upon the lonely moated grange.
　　　　She only said, "My life is dreary,
　　　　　　He cometh not," she said;
　　　　She said, "I am aweary, aweary,
　　　　　　I would that I were dead!"

Her tears fell with the dews at even;
　　Her tears fell ere the dews were dried;
She could not look on the sweet heaven,
　　Either at morn or eventide.
After the flitting of the bats,
　　When thickest dark did trance the sky,
　　She drew her casement-curtain by,
And glanced athwart the glooming flats.
　　　　She only said, "The night is dreary,
　　　　　　He cometh not," she said;
　　　　She said, "I am aweary, aweary,
　　　　　　I would that I were dead!"

Upon the middle of the night,
　　Waking she heard the night-fowl crow:
The cock sung out an hour ere light:
　　From the dark fen the oxen's low

Came to her: without hope of change,
  In sleep she seem'd to walk forlorn,
  Till cold winds woke the gray-eyed morn
About the lonely moated grange.
    She only said, "The day is dreary,
      He cometh not," she said ;
    She said, "I am aweary, aweary,
      I would that I were dead!"

About a stone-cast from the wall
  A sluice with blacken'd waters slept,
And o'er it many, round and small,
  The cluster'd marish-mosses crept.
Hard by a poplar shook alway,
  All silver-green with gnarled bark :
  For leagues no other tree did mark
The level waste, the rounding gray.
    She only said, "My life is dreary,
      He cometh not," she said ;
    She said, "I am aweary, aweary,
      I would that I were dead!"

And ever when the moon was low,
  And the shrill winds were up and away,
In the white curtain, to and fro,
  She saw the gusty shadow sway.
But when the moon was very low,
  And wild winds bound within their cell,
  The shadow of the poplar fell
Upon her bed, across her brow.

> She only said, "The night is dreary,
>   He cometh not," she said;
> She said, "I am aweary, aweary,
>   I would that I were dead!"

All day within the dreamy house,
The doors upon their hinges creak'd;
The blue fly sung in the pane; the mouse
  Behind the mouldering wainscot shriek'd,
Or from the crevice peer'd about.
  Old faces glimmer'd thro' the doors,
  Old footsteps trod the upper floors,
Old voices called her from without.
  She only said, "My life is dreary,
    He cometh not," she said;
  She said, "I am aweary, aweary,
    I would that I were dead!"

The sparrow's chirrup on the roof,
  The slow clock ticking, and the sound
Which to the wooing wind aloof
  The poplar made, did all confound
Her sense; but most she loathed the hour
  When the thick-moted sunbeam lay
  Athwart the chambers, and the day
Was sloping toward his western bower.
  Then, said she, "I am very dreary,
    He will not come," she said;
  She wept, "I am aweary, aweary,
    Oh God, that I were dead!"

Lord Tennyson.

A New Year Carol

HERE we bring new water from
    the well so clear,
For to worship God with, this
    happy New Year;
Sing levy dew, sing levy dew, the
    water and the wine,
With seven bright gold wires,
    and bugles that do shine;
Sing reign of fair maid with
    gold upon her toe,
Open you the West door, and
    turn the Old Year go;
Sing reign of fair maid with gold
    upon her chin,
Open you the East door and
    turn the New Year in.

Anonymous.

The Fairies' Farewell

FAREWELL rewards and Fairies!
    Good housewives now may say;
For now foule sluts in dairies
    Doe fare as well as they;
And though they sweepe their hearths no less
    Than mayds were wont to doe,
Yet who of late for cleaneliness
    Finds sixe-pence in her shoe?

Lament, lament old Abbies,
   The fairies lost command ;
They did but change priests babies,
   But some have chang'd your land ;
And all your children stoln from thence
   And now growne Puritanes,
Who live as changelings ever since,
   For love of your demaines.

At morning and at evening both
   You merry were and glad,
So little care of sleepe and sloth
   These prettie ladies had.
When Tom came home from labour
   Or Ciss to milking rose,
Then merrily went their tabour,
   And nimbly went their toes.

Witness those rings and roundelayes
   Of theirs, which yet remaine ;
Were footed in Queen Maries dayes
   On many a grassy playne.
But since of late Elizabeth
   And later James came in,
They never danced on any heath,
   As when the time hath bin.

By which wee note the fairies
   Were of the old profession ;
Their songs were *Ave Maries*,
   Their dances were procession.

But now, alas! they all are dead,
　Or gone beyond the seas,
Or farther for religion fled,
　Or else they take their ease.

A tell-tale in their company
　They never could endure;
And whoso kept not secretly
　Their mirth was punish'd sure;
It was a just and christian deed
　To pinch such blacke and blue:
O how the common-welth doth need
　Such justices as you!

Now they have left our quarters;
　A Register they have
Who can preserve their charters;
　A man both wise and grave.
An hundred of their merry pranks
　By one that I could name
Are kept in store; con twenty thanks
　To William for the same.

To William Churne of Staffordshire
　Give laud and praises due,
Who every meale can mend your cheare
　With tales both old and true;
To William all give audience,
　And pray yee for his noddle,
For all the fairies evidence
　Were lost, if it were addle.

Richard Corbet.

Drinking Songs

I

>Back and side go bare, go bare,
>   Both foot and hand go cold ;
>But belly, God send thee good ale enough ;
>   Whether it be new or old !

I cannot eat but little meat ; my stomach is not good ;
But, sure, I think that I can drink with him that wears a hood.
Though I go bare ; take ye no care, I am nothing acold ;
I stuff my skin so full within of jolly good ale and old.
   Back and side go bare, go bare, etc.

I love no roast but a nut-brown toast, and a crab laid in the fire ;
A little bread shall do me stead ! much bread I do not desire ;
No frost, nor snow, no wind, I trow, can hurt me if I would ;
I am so wrapped, and throughly lapped of jolly good ale and old !
   Back and side go bare, go bare, etc.

And Tyb my Wife, that as her life loveth well good ale to seek,
Full oft drinks she, till ye may see the tears run down her cheek ;

Then doth she troll to me the bowl, even as a Malt
   Worm should ;
And saith, "Sweet Heart! I took my part of this
   jolly good ale and old!"
   　　Back and side go bare, go bare, etc.

Now let them drink till they nod and wink, even as
   Good Fellows should do,
They shall not miss to have the bliss good ale doth
   bring men to.
And all poor souls that have scoured bowls, or have
   them lustily trolled,
God save the lives of them and their Wives, whether
   they be young or old !
   　　Back and side go bare, go bare, etc.

   　　John Still, Bishop of Bath and Wells.

II

When as the chill Charokko blows,
   And Winter tells a heavy tale ;
When pyes and daws and rooks and crows
Sit cursing of the frosts and snows ;
   Then give me ale.

Ale in a Saxon rumkin then,
   Such as will make grimalkin prate ;
Bids valour burgeon in tall men,
Quickens the poet's wit and pen,
   Despises fate.

Ale, that the absent battle fights,
   And frames the march of Swedish drum,
Disputes with princes, laws, and rights,
What's done and past tells mortal wights,
   And what's to come.

Ale, that the plowman's heart up-keeps
   And equals it with tyrants' thrones,
That wipes the eye that over-weeps,
And lulls in sure and dainty sleeps
   Th' o'er-wearied bones.

Grandchild of Ceres, Bacchus' daughter,
   Wine's emulous neighbour, though but stale,
Ennobling all the nymphs of water,
And filling each man's heart with laughter—
   Ha! give me ale!

Anonymous.

Written at an Inn at Henley

TO thee, fair freedom, I retire
   From flattery, cards, and dice, and din;
Nor art thou found in mansions higher
   Than the low cot or humble inn.

'Tis here with boundless power I reign,
   And every health which I begin
Converts dull port to bright champagne:
   Such freedom crowns it at an inn.

I fly from pomp, I fly from plate,
  I fly from falsehood's specious grin;
Freedom I love, and form I hate,
  And choose my lodgings at an inn.

Here, waiter! take my sordid ore,
  Which lackeys else might hope to win;
It buys what courts have not in store,
  It buys one freedom at an inn.

Whoe'er has travelled life's dull round,
  Where'er his stages may have been,
May sigh to think he still has found
  The warmest welcome at an inn.

William Shenstone.

The Village Shop

HERE, as each season yields a different store,
  Each season's stores in order ranged been,
Apples with cabbage net y-covered o'er,
Calling full sore th' unmoneyed wight, are seen,
And gooseb'rie, clad in liv'ry red or green:
And here of lovely dye the Catherine pear,
Fine pear! as lovely for thy juice I ween:
O may no wight e'er pennyless come there,
Lest smit with ardent love he pine with hopeless care!

See! cherries here, ere cherries yet abound,
With thread so white in tempting posies ty'd,
Scatt'ring like blooming maid their glances round,

With pamp'ring look draw little eyes aside,
And must be bought, though penury betide;
The plum all azure, and the nut all brown.
And here each season do those cakes abide,
Whose honour'd names th' inventive city own,
Rend'ring thro' Britain's isle Salopia's praises
    known.

Admir'd Salopia! that with venial pride
Eyes her bright form in Severn's ambient wave,
Fam'd for her loyal cares in perils try'd,
Her daughters lovely, and her striplings brave:
Ah! midst the rest, may flowers adorn his grave,
Whose art did first these dulcet cakes display!
A motive fair to Learning's imps he gave,
Who cheerless o'er her darkling region stray,
Till Reason's morn arise and light them on their
    way.   *William Shenstone.*

The Hock-cart, or Harvest Home

COME, Sons of Summer, by whose toile,
    We are the Lords of Wine and Oile;
By whose tough labours, and rough hands,
We rip up first, then reap our lands.
Crown'd with the eares of corne, now come,
And, to the Pipe, sing Harvest home.
Come forth, my Lord, and see the Cart
Drest up with all the Country Art.
See, here a Maukin, there a sheet,
As spotlesse pure, as it is sweet:

The Horses, Mares, and frisking Fillies,
(Clad, all, in Linen, white as Lillies.)
The Harvest Swaines, and Wenches bound
For joy, to see the Hock-cart crown'd.
About the Cart, heare, how the Rout
Of Rurall Younglings raise the shout;
Pressing before, some coming after,
Those with a shout, and these with laughter.
Some bless the Cart; some kiss the sheaves;
Some prank them up with Oaken leaves:
Some crosse the Fill-horse; some with great
Devotion, stroak the home-borne wheat:
While other Rusticks, lesse attent
To Prayers, then to Merryment,
Run after with their breeches rent.
Well, on, brave boyes, to your Lord's Hearth,
Glitt'ring with fire; where, for your mirth,
Ye shall see first the large and cheefe
Foundation of your Feast, Fat Beefe:
With Upper Stories, Mutton, Veale
And Bacon, (which makes full the meale)
With sev'rall dishes standing by,
As here a Custard, there a Pie,
And here all-tempting Frumentie.
And for to make the merry cheere,
If smirking Wine be wanting here,
There's that, which drowns all care, stout Beere;
Which freely drink to your Lord's health,
Then to the Plough, (the Common-wealth)
Next to your Flailes, your Fanes, your Fatts;
Then to the Maids with Wheaten Hats:

To the rough Sickle, and crookt Sythe,
Drink, frollick, boyes, till all be blythe.
Feed and grow fat ; and as ye eat,
Be mindfull, that the lab'ring Neat
(As you) may have their fill of meat.
And know, besides, ye must revoke
The patient Oxe unto the Yoke,
And all goe back unto the Plough
And Harrow, (though they'r hang'd up now.)
And, you must know, your Lords words true,
Feed him ye must, whose food fils you.
And that this pleasure is like raine,
Not sent ye for to drowne your paine,
But for to make it spring againe.

Robert Herrick.

Three Drinking Songs

I

THE nut-brown ale, the nut-brown ale,
   Puts down all drink when it is stale !
The toast, the nutmeg, and the ginger
Will make a sighing man a singer.
Ale gives a buffet in the head,
   But ginger under-props the brain ;
When ale would strike a strong man dead
   Then nutmeg tempers it again.
The nut-brown ale, the nut-brown ale,
Puts down all drink when it is stale !

John Marston.

II

A Bee goes mumbling homeward pleased,
　He hath not slaved away his hours ;
He's drunken with a thousand healths
　Of love and kind regards for flowers.
　　　Pour out the wine,
　　　His joy be mine.

Forgetful of affairs at home,
　He hath sipped oft and merrily ;
Forgetful of his duty—Oh !
　What can he say to his queen bee?
　　　He says in wine,
　　　"Boo to her shrine !"

The coward dog that wags his tail,
　And rubs the nose with mangy curs,
And fearful says, "Come, play, not fight,"
　Knows not the draught to drown his fears ;
　　　Knows not the wine,
　　　The ruby shine.

Poor beggar, breathless in yon barn,
　Who fear'st a mouse to move thy straw,
Must conscience pester thee all night,
　And fear oppress with thoughts of law?
　　　O dearth of wine,
　　　No sleep is thine.

Is Bacchus not the god of gods,
　Who gives to Beauty's cheeks their shine?

O Love, thou art a wingless worm ;
  Wouldst thou be winged, fill thee with wine :
      Fill thee with wine,
      And wings be thine.

Then, Bacchus, rule thy merry race,
  And laws like thine who would not keep?
And when fools weep to hear us laugh,
  We'll laugh, ha ! ha ! to see them weep.
      O god of wine,
      My soul be thine.
                  William H. Davies.

III

They sell good beer at Haslemere
  And under Guildford Hill ;
At little Cowfold, as I've been told,
  A beggar may drink his fill.
There is a good brew in Amberley too,
  And by the Bridge also ;
But the swipes they take in at the Washington Inn
  Is the very best beer I know.

    With my here it goes, there it goes,
      All the fun's before us.
    The door's ajar and the barrel is sprung,
    The tipple's aboard and the night is young ;
    I am singing the best song ever was sung,
      And it has a rousing chorus.

If I was what I never can be,
   The Master or the Squire;
If you gave me the rape from here to the sea,
   Which is more than I desire:
Then all my crops should be barley and hops,
   And did my harvest fail,
I'd sell every rood of my acres, I would,
   For a bellyful of good ale.
Hilaire Belloc.

The Milkmaid

WHAT a dainty life the milkmaid leads,
   When over the flowery meads
She dabbles in the dew
And sings to her cow,
And feels not the pain
Of love or disdain!
She sleeps in the night, though she toils in the day,
And merrily passeth her time away.
Thomas Nabbes.

Merry Margaret

MERRY Margaret
   As midsummer flower,
  Gentle as falcon
  Or hawk of the tower:
With solace and gladness,
Much mirth and no madness,
All good and no badness;

      So joyously,
      So maidenly,
      So womanly
      Her demeaning
      In everything,
      Far, far passing
      That I can indite,
      Or suffice to write
Of Merry Margaret
As midsummer flower,
Gentle as falcon
Or hawk of the tower.
As patient and still
And as full of good will
As fair Isaphill,
Coliander,
Sweet pomander,
Good Cassander ;
Steadfast of thought,
Well made, well wrought,
Far may be sought,
Ere that ye can find
So courteous, so kind,
As Merry Margaret,
This midsummer flower,
Gentle as falcon
Or hawk of the tower.

John Skelton.

The Village Schoolmistress

ONE ancient hen she took delight to feed,
  The plodding pattern of the busy dame,
Which ever and anon, impell'd by need,
Into her school, begirt with chickens, came,
Such favour did her past deportment claim;
And if neglect had lavish'd on the ground
Fragment of bread, she would collect the same:
For well she knew, and quaintly could expound,
What sin it were to waste the smallest crumb she found.

Herbs, too, she knew, and well of each could speak,
That in her garden sipp'd the silv'ry dew,
Where no vain flow'r disclos'd a gaudy streak,
But herbs for use, and physic, not a few,
Of grey renown, within those borders grew;
The tufted basil, pun-provoking thyme,
Fresh baum, and marygold of cheerful hue,
The lowly gill, that never dares to climb,
And more I fain would sing, disdaining here to rhyme.

Yet euphrasy may not be left unsung,
That gives dim eyes to wander leagues around,
And pungent radish, biting infant's tongue,
And plaintain ribb'd, that heals the reaper's wound,
And marj'ram sweet, in shepherd's posie found,
And lavender, whose pikes of azure bloom
Shall be, erewhile, in arid bundles bound,

To lurk amidst the labours of her loom,
And crown her kerchief clean with mickle rare
    perfume.

And here trim rosemarie, that whilom crown'd
The daintiest garden of the proudest peer,
Ere, driven from its envy'd site, it found
A sacred shelter for its branches here,
Where edged with gold its glitt'ring skirts appear.
O wassel days! O customs meet and well!
Ere this was banish'd from its lofty sphere;
Simplicity then sought this humble cell,
Nor ever would she more with thane and lordling
    dwell. *William Shenstone.*

The Solitary Reaper

BEHOLD her, single in the field,
    Yon solitary Highland Lass!
Reaping and singing by herself;
Stop here, or gently pass!
Alone she cuts and binds the grain,
And sings a melancholy strain;
O listen! for the Vale profound
Is overflowing with the sound.

No Nightingale did ever chaunt
More welcome notes to weary bands
Of travellers in some shady haunt,
Among Arabian sands:

A voice so thrilling ne'er was heard
In Spring-time from the Cuckoo-bird,
Breaking the silence of the seas
Among the farthest Hebrides.

Will no one tell me what she sings?—
Perhaps the plaintive numbers flow
For old, unhappy, far-off things,
And battles long ago:
Or is it some more humble lay,
Familiar matter of to-day?
Some natural sorrow, loss, or pain,
That has been, and may be again !

Whate'er the theme, the Maiden sang
As if her song could have no ending ;
I saw her singing at her work,
And o'er the sickle bending ;—
I listened till I had my fill ;
And, as I mounted up the hill,
The music in my heart I bore,
Long after it was heard no more.

William Wordsworth.

From "The Steele Glasse"

BEHOLD him, priests, and though he stink of sweat,
Disdain him not, for shall I tell you what?
Such climb to heaven before the shaven crowns.
But how? Forsooth, with true humility.

Not that they hoard their grain when it is cheap,
Not that they kill the calf to have the milk,
Not that they set debate between their lords,
By earing up the balks that part their bounds;
Nor for because they can both crouch and creep
(The guileful'st men that ever God yet made)
When as they mean most mischief and deceit;
Not that they can cry out on landlords loud,
And say they rack their rents an ace too high
When they themselves do sell their landlord's lamb
For greater price than ewe was wont be worth.
But for they feed with fruits of their great pains
Both King and Knight and Priests in cloister pent.
Therefore I say that sooner some of them
Shall scale the walls which lead us up to heaven,
Than corn-fed beasts, whose belly is their God,
Although they preach of more perfection.

George Gascoigne.

The Leech Gatherer

THERE was a roaring in the wind all night;
   The rain came heavily and fell in floods;
But now the sun is rising calm and bright;
The birds are singing in the distant woods;
Over his own sweet voice the Stock-dove broods;
The Jay makes answer as the Magpie chatters;
And all the air is filled with pleasant noise of
   waters.

All things that love the sun are out of doors;
The sky rejoices in the morning's birth;
The grass is bright with rain-drops;—on the moors
The Hare is running races in her mirth;
Aud with her feet she from the plashy earth
Raises a mist; that, glittering in the sun,
Runs with her all the way, wherever she doth run.

I was a traveller then upon the moor;
I saw the Hare that raced about with joy;
I heard the woods and distant waters roar;
Or heard them not, as happy as a boy:
The pleasant season did my heart employ:
My old remembrances went from me wholly;
And all the ways of men, so vain and melancholy!

But, as it sometimes chanceth, from the might
Of joy in minds that can no further go,
As high as we have mounted in delight
In our dejection do we sink as low,
To me that morning did it happen so;
And fears and fancies thick upon me came;
Dim sadness—and blind thoughts, I knew not, nor
    could name.

I heard the Sky-lark warbling in the sky;
And I bethought me of the playful Hare:
Even such a happy child of earth am I;
Even as these blissful creatures do I fare;
Far from the world I walk, and from all care;
But there may come another day to me—
Solitude, pain of heart, distress, and poverty.

My whole life I have lived in pleasant thought,
As if life's business were a summer mood:
As if all needful things would come unsought
To genial faith, still rich in genial good:
But how can He expect that others should
Build for him, sow for him, and at his call
Love him, who for himself will take no heed at all?

I thought of Chatterton, the marvellous Boy,
The sleepless Soul that perished in his pride;
Of Him who walked in glory and in joy
Following his plough, along the mountain-side:
By our own spirits are we deified;
We Poets in our youth begin in gladness;
But thereof comes in the end despondency and
    madness.

Now, whether it were by peculiar grace,
A leading from above, a something given,
Yet it befel, that, in this lonely place,
When I with these untoward thoughts had striven,
Beside a pool bare to the eye of heaven
I saw a Man before me unawares:
The oldest man he seemed that ever wore grey hairs.

As a huge Stone is sometimes seen to lie
Couched on the bald top of an eminence;
Wonder to all who do the same espy,
By what means it could thither come, and whence,
So that it seems a thing endued with sense:
Like a Sea-beast crawled forth, that on a shelf
Of rock or sand reposeth, there to sun itself;

Such seemed this Man, not all alive nor dead,
Nor all asleep—in his extreme old age:
His body was bent double, feet and head
Coming together in life's pilgrimage;
As if some dire constraint of pain, or rage
Of sickness felt by him in times long past,
A more than human weight upon his frame had cast.

Himself he propped, his body, limbs, and face,
Upon a long grey Staff of shaven wood:
And, still as I drew near with gentle pace,
Upon the margin of that moorish flood
Motionless as a Cloud the Old-man stood;
That heareth not the loud winds when they call;
And moveth all together, if it move at all.

At length, himself unsettling, he the Pond
Stirred with his staff, and fixedly did look
Upon the muddy water, which he conned,
As if he had been reading in a book:
And now a stranger's privilege I took;
And, drawing to his side, to him did say,
"This morning gives us promise of a glorious day."

A gentle answer did the Old-man make,
In courteous speech which forth he slowly drew:
And him with further words I thus bespake,
"What occupation do you there pursue?
This is a lonesome place for one like you."
He answered, while a flash of mild surprise
Broke from the sable orbs of his yet vivid eyes.

His words came feebly, from a feeble chest,
But each in solemn order followed each,
With something of a lofty utterance drest—
Choice word and measured phrase, above the reach
Of ordinary men; a stately speech;
Such as grave livers do in Scotland use,
Religious men, who give to God and Man their dues.

He told, that to these waters he had come
To gather Leeches, being old and poor:
Employment hazardous and wearisome!
And he had many hardships to endure;
From pond to pond he roamed, from moor to moor;
Housing, with God's good help, by choice or chance;
And in this way he gained an honest maintenance.

The Old-man still stood talking by my side;
But now his voice to me was like a stream
Scarce heard; nor word from word could I divide;
And the whole Body of the Man did seem
Like one whom I had met with in a dream;
Or like a man from some far region sent,
To give me human strength, by apt admonishment.

My former thoughts returned: the fear that kills;
And hope that is unwilling to be fed;
Cold, pain, and labour; and all fleshly ills;
And mighty Poets in their misery dead.
—Perplexed, and longing to be comforted,
My question eagerly did I renew,
"How is it that you live, and what is it you do?"

He with a smile did then his words repeat;
And said, that, gathering Leeches, far and wide
He travelled; stirring thus about his feet
The waters of the Pools where they abide.
"Once I could meet with them on every side;
But they have dwindled long by slow decay;
Yet still I persevere, and find them where I may."

While he was talking thus, the lonely place,
The Old-man's shape, and speech, all troubled me:
In my mind's eye I seemed to see him pace
About the weary moors continually,
Wandering about alone and silently.
While I these thoughts within myself pursued,
He, having made a pause, the same discourse renewed.

And soon with this he other matter blended,
Cheerfully uttered, with demeanour kind,
But stately in the main; and when he ended,
I could have laughed myself to scorn to find
In that decrepit Man so firm a mind.
"God," said I, "be my help and stay secure;
I'll think of the Leech-gatherer on the lonely moor!"

William Wordsworth.

Animals

I THINK I could turn and live with animals, they are so placid and self-contained.
I stand and look at them sometimes half the day long.

They do not sweat and whine about their condition,
They do not lie awake in the dark and weep for
   their sins,
They do not make me sick discussing their duty to
   God,
No one is dissatisfied, not one is demented with the
   mania of owning things,
Not one kneels to another, nor to his kind that
   lived thousands of years ago,
Not one is respectable or industrious over the whole
   earth.
So they show their relations to me, and I accept
   them,
They bring me tokens of myself, they evince them
   plainly in their possession.
                                    Walt Whitman.

The White Island

IN this world, the Isle of Dreams,
   While we sit by sorrow's streams,
Tears and terrors are our themes,
      Reciting:

But when once from hence we fly,
More and more approaching nigh
Unto young eternity,
      Uniting —
In that whiter Island, where
Things are evermore sincere;
Candour here, and lustre there,

    Delighting :—
There no monstrous fancies shall
Out of hell an horror call
To create, or cause at all
    Affrighting :
There, in calm and cooling sleep,
We our eyes shall never steep,
But eternal watch shall keep,
    Attending
Pleasures such as shall pursue
Me immortalized, and you ;
And fresh joys, as never too
    Have ending. *Robert Herrick.*

Welcome

'TIS late and cold ; stir up the fire :
    Sit close, and draw the table nigher ;
Be merry, and drink wine that's old,
A hearty medicine 'gainst a cold :
Your beds of wanton down the best,
Where you shall tumble to your rest ;
I could wish you wenches too,
But I am dead, and cannot do.
Call for the best the house may ring,
Sack, white, and claret let them bring,
And drink apace, while breath you have ;
You'll find but cold drink in the grave :
Plover, partridge, for your dinner,
And a capon for the sinner,

You shall find ready when you're up,
And your horse shall have his sup:
Welcome, welcome, shall fly round,
And I shall smile, though underground.

John Fletcher.

Come, Sweet Lass

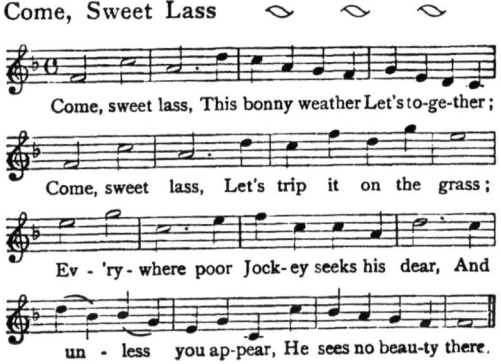

Come, sweet lass, This bonny weather Let's to-ge-ther;
Come, sweet lass, Let's trip it on the grass;
Ev-'ry-where poor Jock-ey seeks his dear, And
un-less you ap-pear, He sees no beau-ty there.

II

On our green
  The loons are sporting,
  Piping, courting;
On our green
  The blithest lads are seen;
There all day
Our lasses dance and play,
And every one is gay,
But I, when you're away.

Sledburn Fair

Lancashire

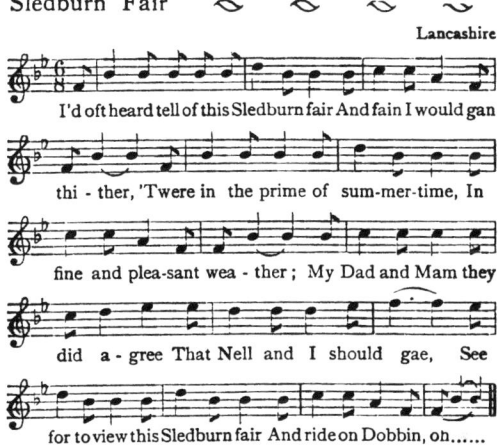

I'd oft heard tell of this Sledburn fair And fain I would gan thi-ther, 'Twere in the prime of sum-mer-time, In fine and plea-sant wea - ther; My Dad and Mam they did a - gree That Nell and I should gae, See for to view this Sledburn fair And ride on Dobbin, oh......

II

So Nell gat on and I gat on,
   And we both rode off together,
And of everybody we did meet
   Enquired how far 'twas thither?
Until we came to t'other field end,
   'Twas about steeple high,
"See yonder, Nell, see yonder, Nell,
   There's Sledburn town," cried I.

III

And when we reached this famous town
   We enquired for an alehouse,
We lookéd up and saw a sign
   As high as any gallows ;

We called for Harry, the ostler,
    To give our horse some hay,
For we had come to Sledburn Fair
    And meant to stop all day.

IV

The landlord then he came out
    And led us up an entry;
He took us in the finest room
    As if we'd been quite gentry.
And puddings and sauce they did so smell,
    Pies and roast beef so rare,
"Oh, Zooks!" says Nell, "we've acted well
    In coming to Sledburn Fair."

Dicky of Taunton Dean

From "Folk Songs from Somerset." Edited by
Cecil Sharp and Charles L. Marson

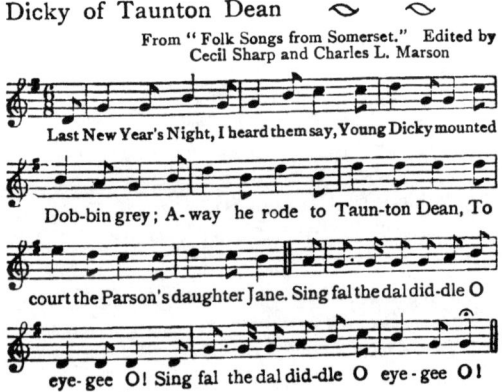

Last New Year's Night, I heard them say, Young Dicky mounted Dob-bin grey; A-way he rode to Taun-ton Dean, To court the Parson's daughter Jane. Sing fal the dal did-dle O eye-gee O! Sing fal the dal did-dle O eye-gee O!

II

His buckskin breeches he put on,
His Sunday clothes so neatly shone:
The hat that he wore on his head
Was neatly trimmed with ribbons red.
    Sing, etc.

III

Away he trotted, and much he sweat
When he came nigh to the Parson's gate:
And there he cried: Hullo! Hullo!
What? Are the good people at home or no?
    Sing, etc.

IV

The trusty servant let him in,
And then the courtship did begin:
Straightway he went into the hall
And aloud for Parson's Jane did call.
    Sing, etc.

V

Miss Jane walked down all in a great sway,
To hear what Dicky had got for to say:
I am a good fellow although I'm poor;
I never did fall in love before.
    Sing, etc.

VI

If I consent to be your bride,
What will you for me provide?
For I can neither card nor spin,
Nor neither help your harvest in.
    Sing, etc.

VII

Sometimes I reap, I plough, I sow,
And sometimes I to the market go:
The old mare's keep be corn and hay,
And she earns me sixpence every day.
    Sing, etc.

VIII

Sixpence a day will never do
To gird me in silks and satins too,
Besides a coach when I take the air—
Whoa ho! says Dicky: You make me stare.
    Sing, etc.

IX

Sixpence a day, that wont find meat,
But faith, says Dick, there be sacks of wheat;
And if you consent for to marry me now,
I'll feed you as fat as father's old sow.
    Sing, etc.

X

His compliments were so polite,
They made the good people laugh outright;
So when young Dick had no more to say,
He mounted on Dobbin and rode away.
    Sing fal the dal diddle O eye-gee O!

Jack and Joan

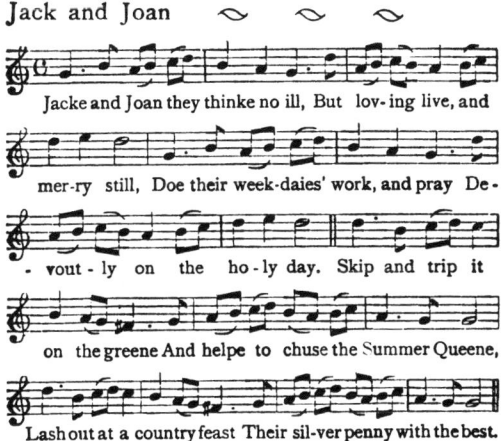

Jacke and Joan they thinke no ill, But lov-ing live, and mer-ry still, Doe their week-daies' work, and pray De-vout-ly on the ho-ly day. Skip and trip it on the greene And helpe to chuse the Summer Queene, Lash out at a country feast Their sil-ver penny with the best.

II

Well can they judge of nappy Ale,
And tell at large a Winter tale,
Climb up to the Apple loft
And turne the Crabs till they be soft
Tib is all the father's joy,
And little Tom the mother's boy:
All their pleasure is content
And care to pay their yearly rent.

III

Jone can call by name her cowes,
And decke her windowes with green boughs,
She can wreathes and tuttyes make
And trim with plums a Bridall Cake.

Jacke knowes what brings gaine or losse,
And his long Flaile can stoutly tosse,
Make the hedge which others breake;
And ever thinkes what he doth speake.

IV

Now you Courtly Dames and Knights,
That study onely strange delights,
Though you scorne the home spun gray
And revell in your rich array,
Though your tongues dissemble deepe,
And can your heads from danger keepe,
Yet, for all your pompe and traine,
Securer lives the silly swaine.

Thomas Campion.

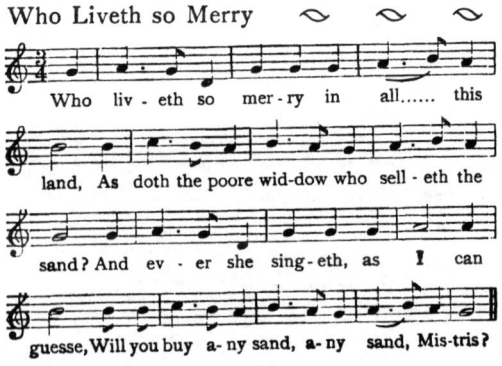

Who liveth so merry in all...... this land, As doth the poore wid-dow who sell-eth the sand? And ev-er she sing-eth, as I can guesse, Will you buy a-ny sand, a-ny sand, Mis-tris?

II

The Broom-man maketh his living most sweet
By carrying of broomes from street to street.
Who would desire a pleasanter thing
Than all the day long to do nothing but sing?

III

The Chimney-sweeper, all the long day
He singeth and sweepeth the soote away.
Yet when he comes home, although he be weary,
With his sweet wife he maketh full merry.

IV

The Cobbler he sits cobling till noone,
And cobbleth his shoes till they be done.
Yet doth he not feare—and so doth say—
For he knowes his work will soon decay.

V

The Marchant-man doth saile on the seas
And lye on the ship-board with little ease.
Always in doubt the rock is near,
How can he be merry and make good cheare?

VI

The Husband-man all day goeth to plow,
And when he comes home he serveth his sow.
He moyleth and toyleth all the long yeare;
How can he be merry and make good cheare?

VII

The Serving-man waiteth from street to street
With blowing his nailes and beating his feet,
And serveth for forty shillings a yeare,
That 'tis impossible to make good cheare.

VIII

Who liveth so merry and maketh such sport
As those that be of the poorest sort?
The poorest sort, wheresoever they be,
They gatner together by one, two and three.
And every man will spend his penny;
What such a shot among a great many?

Poor Old Horse

Westmorland

My clothing was once of the linsey woolsey fine, My tail it grew at length, My coat did likewise shine; But now I'm growing old My beauty does decay, My master frowns upon me; One day I heard him say, "Poor old horse, poor old horse."

II

Once I was kept in the stable snug and warm,
To keep my tender limbs from any cold or harm;
But now, in open fields, I am forced for to go,
In all sorts of weather, let it be hail, rain, freeze, or snow.

III

Once I was fed on the very best corn and hay
That ever grew in yon fields, or in yon meadows gay;
But now there's no such doing can I find at all,
I'm glad to pick the green sprouts that grow behind yon wall.

IV

You are old, you are cold, you are deaf, dull, dumb and slow,
You are not fit for anything, or in my team to draw,
You have eaten all my hay, you have spoiled all my straw,
So hang him, whip him, stick him, to the huntsman let him go.

V

My hide unto the tanners then I would freely give,
My body to the hound dogs, I would rather die than live,
Likewise my poor old bones that have carried you many a mile,
Over hedges, ditches, brooks and bridges, likewise gates and stiles.

Chorus. Poor old horse, poor old horse.

Meum est Propositum

Welsh air: "Nos Galan"

Me - um est pro - po - si - tum in ta - ber - na mo - ri Vi - num sit ap - po - si - tum si - ti - en - ti o - ri Ut di - cant cum vi - der - int an - gel - or - um cho - ri De - us sit pro - pi - ti - us hu - ic po - ta - to - ri.

II

Potatores singuli
  Sunt omnes benigni;
Tam senes quam juvenes;
  In aeterna igni
Cruciantur rustici,
  Qui non sunt tam digni
Qui bibisse noverint
  Bonum vinum vini.

III

Vinum super omnia
  Bonum diligamus,
Nam purgantur vissia,
  Dum vinum potamus;

Cum nobis sit copia,
 Vinum dum clamamus,
Qui vivis in gloria
 Te Deum laudamus ...

IV

Magis quam ecclesiam
 Diligo tabernam,
Ipsam nullo tempore
 Sprevi neque spernam,
Donec sanctos angelos
 Venientes cernam,
Cantantes pro ebriis
 Requiem aternam.

Salt Beef

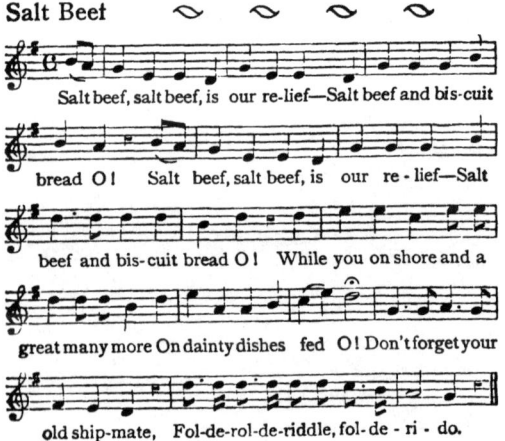

Salt beef, salt beef, is our re-lief—Salt beef and bis-cuit bread O! Salt beef, salt beef, is our re-lief—Salt beef and bis-cuit bread O! While you on shore and a great many more On dainty dishes fed O! Don't forget your old ship-mate, Fol-de-rol-de-riddle, fol-de-ri-do.

II

Our hammocks they swing wet and cold,
But in them we must lie O !   (*bis*)
While you on shore, and a great many more,
Are sleeping warm and dry O !
Don't forget your old shipmate.
Fol-de-rol-de-riddle-fol-de-ri-do.

The "Princess Royal"

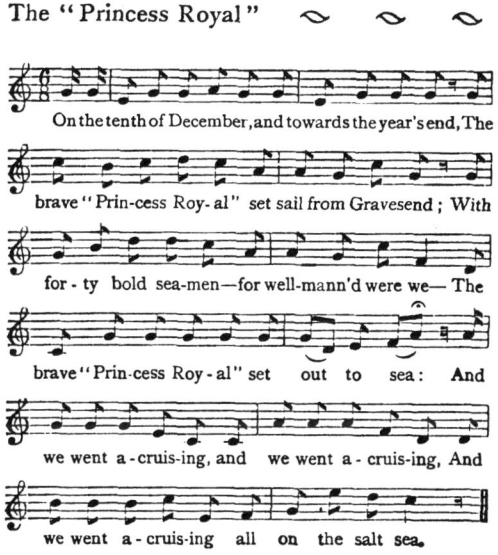

On the tenth of December, and towards the year's end, The brave "Prin-cess Roy-al" set sail from Gravesend ; With for-ty bold sea-men—for well-mann'd were we— The brave "Prin-cess Roy-al" set out to sea : And we went a-cruis-ing, and we went a-cruis-ing, And we went a-cruis-ing all on the salt sea.

II

We had not been cruising for days twenty-three
When a man at the masthead a vessel spied he.
She bore down upon us with sails hoisted high,
And under her mizzen black colours did fly.
  And we, etc.

III

An hour or two after he bore alongside:
With a loud speaking trumpet: "Whence come you?" he cried.
"We come from Giberaltar and bound to Peru."
"Then back your main topsail and heave your ship to,
And we'll go a cruising, etc., alongside of you."

IV

"We'll back our main topsail and heave our ship to;
But that in some harbour, not alongside of you."
So we hoisted the royals and set the topsail,
And the bold "Princess Royal" soon showed them her tail.
  And we, etc.

Soldiers Three

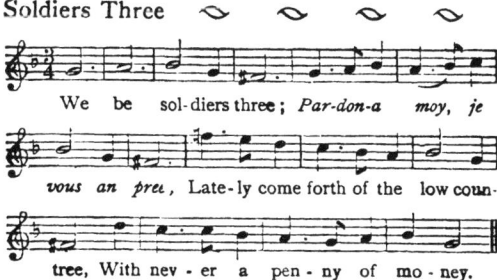

We be soldiers three; *Pardon-a moy, je vous an preu,* Lately come forth of the low countree, With never a penny of money.

II

Here, good fellow, I drinke to thee, Pardona moy, je vous, an pree,
And to all good fellowes, whoever they be, With never a penny of money.

III

And he that will not pledge me this, Pardona moy, je vous, an pree,
Pays for the shot, whatever it is, With never a penny of money.

IV

Charge it againe, boy, charge it againe, Pardona moy, je vous, an pree,
As long as there is any ink in thy pen, With never a penny of money.

THE FOOTPATH

To Violets

WELCOME, maids-of-honour,
    You do bring
    In the Spring,
And wait upon her.

She has virgins many,
    Fresh and fair;
    Yet you are
More sweet than any.

You're the maiden posies,
    And so graced
    To be placed
'Fore damask roses.

Yet, though thus respected,
    By and by
    Ye do lie
Poor girls, neglected.

Robert Herrick.

Sweet Bird

SWEET bird, that sing'st away the early hours,
  Of winters past, or coming, void of care,
Well pleased with delights which present are,
Fair seasons, budding sprays, sweet-smelling flowers:

To rocks, to springs, to rills, from leafy bowers
Thou thy Creator's goodness dost declare,
And what dear gifts in thee he did not spare,
A stain to human sense in sin that lowers.
What soul can be so sick, which by thy songs
(Attir'd in sweetness) sweetly is not driven
Quite to forget Earth's turmoils, spites, and wrongs,
And lift a reverent eye and thought to Heaven?
Sweet, artless songster, thou my mind dost raise
To airs of spheres, yea, and to angels' lays.

William Drummond.

The Plougher

SUNSET and silence; a man; around him earth savage, earth broken:
Beside him two horses, a plough!
Earth savage, earth broken, the brutes, the dawn-man there in the sunset!
And the plough that is twin to the sword, that is founder of cities!
"Brute-tamer, plough-maker, earth-breaker! Can'st hear? There are ages between us!
Is it praying you are as you stand there, alone in the sunset?
Surely our sky-born gods can be nought to you, Earth-child and Earth-master!
Surely your thoughts are of Pan, or of Wotan or Dana!
Yet why give thought to the gods? Has Pan led your brutes where they stumble?

Has Wotan put hands to your plough or Dana
numbed pain of the childbed?
What matter your foolish reply, O man standing
lone and bowed earthward.
Your task is a day near its close. Give thanks to
the night-giving God."
Slowly the darkness falls, the broken lands blend
with the savage,
The brute-tamer stands by the brutes, by a head's
breadth only above them!
A head's breadth, ay, but therein is Hell's depth
and the height up to Heaven,
And the thrones of the gods, and their halls and
their chariots, purples and splendours.

Padraic Colum.

A Faery Song ⌇ ⌇ ⌇

Sung by the people of Faery over Diarmiud and Grania, who lay in their bridal sleep under a cromlech.

WE who are old, old and gay,
   O so old!
Thousands of years, thousands of years,
If all were told,

Give to these children, new from the world,
Silence and love;
And the long dew-dropping hours of the night,
And the stars above:

Give to these children, new from the world,
Rest far from men.
Is anything better, anything better?
Tell us it then:

Us who are old, old and gay:
O so old!
Thousands of years, thousands of years,
If all were told.
W. B. Yeats.

Lines from the "Milton"
of William Blake

THOU hearest the Nightingale begin the Song
of Spring;
The lark sitting upon his earthy bed, just as the morn
Appears, listens silent, then springing from the waving Corn-field, loud
He leads the Choir of Day—trill, trill, trill, trill,
Mounting upon the wing of light into the Great Expanse,
Re-echoing against the lovely blue and shining heavenly Shell,
His little throat labours with inspiration; every feather
On throat and breast and wings vibrates with the effluence Divine.

All Nature listens silent to him, and the awful Sun
Stands still upon the Mountain looking on this
    little Bird
With eyes of soft humility and wonder, love, and
    awe.

The Birch-tree at Loschwitz

AT Loschwitz above the city
    The air is sunny and chill;
The birch-trees and the pine-trees
    Grow thick upon the hill.

Lone and tall, with silver stem,
    A birch-tree stands apart;
The passionate wind of spring-time
    Stirs in its leafy heart.

I lean against the birch-tree,
    My arms around it twine;
It pulses, and leaps, and quivers,
    Like a human heart to mine.

One moment I stand, then sudden
    Let loose mine arms that cling:
O God! the lonely hillside,
    The passionate wind of spring!

Amy Levy.

Atavism

DEEP in the jungle vast and dim,
    That knew not a white man's feet,
I smelt the odour of sun-warmed fur,
    Musky, savage and sweet.

Far it was from the huts of men
    And the grass where Sambur feed;
I threw a stone at a Kadapu tree
    That bled as a man might bleed.

Scent of fur and colour of blood:—
    And the long-dead instincts rose,
I followed the lure of my season's mate,—
    And flew, bare-fanged, at my foes.

   .   .   .   .   .   .

Pale days: and a league of laws
    Made by the whims of men.
Would I were back with my furry cubs
    In the dusk of a jungle den.

Laurence Hope ("Indian Love": Heinemann).

Ca' the Yowes to the Knowes

Ca' the yowes to the knowes,
    Ca' them where the heather grows,
Ca' them where the burnie rows,
    My bonnie dearie.

As I gaed down the water side,
There I met my shepherd lad;
He row'd me sweetly in his plaid,
    And he ca'd me his dearie

" Will ye gang down the water side,
And see the waves sae sweetly glide
Beneath the hazels spreading wide?
    The moon it shines fu' clearly."

I was bred up at nae sic school,
My shepherd lad, to play the fool,
And a' the day to sit in dool,
    And naebody to see me."

" Ye sall get gowns and ribbons meet,
Cauf-leather shoon upon your feet,
And in my arms ye'se lie and sleep,
    And ye sall be my dearie."

" If ye'll but stand to what ye've said,
I'se gang wi' you, my shepherd lad,
And ye may row me in your plaid,
    And I sall be your dearie."

" While waters wimple to the sea,
While day blinks in the lift sae hie,
Till clay-cauld death sall blin' my e'e,
    Ye aye sall be my dearie!"

Isobel Pagan.

The Harbour

STEER hither, steer your winged pines,
    All-beaten mariners!
Here lie Love's undiscovered mines,
    A prey to passengers;
Perfumes far sweeter than the best
Which make the Phœnix' urn and nest.
    Fear not your ships,
Nor any to oppose you save our lips;
    But come on shore
Where no joy dies till love hath gotten more

For swelling waves our panting breasts,
    Where never storms arise,
Exchange, and be awhile our guests;
    For stars gaze on our eyes.
The compass love shall hourly sing,
And as he goes about the ring,
    We will not miss
To tell each point he nameth with a kiss.
    Then come on shore,
Where no joy dies till love hath gotten more.

                                     William Browne

O'er the Moor amang the Heather

COMING through the craigs o' Kyle,
    Amang the bonnie blooming heather,
There I met a bonnie lassie,
   Keeping a' her ewes thegither.

O'er the moor amang the heather,
   O'er the moor amang the heather;
There I met a bonnie lassie,
   Keeping a' her ewes thegither.

Says I, my dear, where is thy hame,—
   In moor or dale, pray tell me whether?
She says, I tend the fleecy flocks
   That feed amang the blooming heather.

We laid us down upon a bank,
   Sae warm and sunny was the weather:
She left her flocks at large to rove
   Amang the bonnie blooming heather.

While thus we lay, she sang a sang,
   Till echo rang a mile and farther;
And aye the burden of the sang
   Was, o'er the moor amang the heather.

She charmed my heart, and aye sinsyne
   I couldna' think on ony ither;
By sea and sky, she shall be mine,
   The bonnie lass amang the heather!

O'er the moor amang the heather,
   Down amang the blooming heather,—
By sea and sky she shall be mine,
   The bonnie lass amang the heather!

Jean Glover.

Remembered Spring

SITTING high on a hill, towards battle is turned
My mind, yet it cannot drive me on.

Sharp is the wind; it is punishment to be alive;
When the trees do on the gay colours
Of Summer, sick exceedingly am I to-day.
I am not a hunter, I keep no hound:
I cannot get about:
As long as she will, let the cuckoo sing.

At Aber Cuawg the cuckoos sing
On the blossoming branches:
Woe to the sick man that hears their jolly notes.

At Aber Cuawg the cuckoos sing.
There are some that hear them and will not hear them again.

Did not I once listen to the cuckoo on the ivied tree?
Did I not bear a shield?
What I loved is but a moan; what I loved is no more. From the Welsh of *Llywarch Hên.*

The Lady of Shalott

Part I

ON either side the river lie
Long fields of barley and of rye,
That clothe the wold and meet the sky;
And thro' the field the road runs by

    To many-tower'd Camelot;
And up and down the people go,
Gazing where the lilies blow
Round an island there below,
    The island of Shalott.

Willows whiten, aspens quiver,
Little breezes dusk and shiver
Thro' the wave that runs for ever
By the island in the river
    Flowing down to Camelot.
Four gray walls, and four gray towers,
Overlook a space of flowers,
And the silent isle embowers
    The Lady of Shalott.

By the margin, willow-veil'd,
Slide the heavy barges trail'd
By slow horses; and unhail'd
The shallop flitteth silken sail'd
    Skimming down to Camelot:
But who hath seen her wave her hand?
Or at the casement seen her stand?
Or is she known in all the land,
    The Lady of Shalott?

Only reapers, reaping early
In among the bearded barley,
Hear a song that echoes cheerly
From the river winding clearly,

>Down to tower'd Camelot:
And by the moon the reaper weary,
Piling sheaves in uplands airy,
Listening, whispers "'Tis the fairy
>   Lady of Shalott."

Part II

There she weaves by night and day
A magic web with colours gay.
She has heard a whisper say,
A curse is on her if she stay
>   To look down to Camelot.
She knows not what the curse may be,
And so she weaveth steadily,
And little other care hath she,
>   The Lady of Shalott.

And moving thro' a mirror clear
That hangs before her all the year,
Shadows of the world appear.
There she sees the highway near
>   Winding down to Camelot:
There the river eddy whirls,
And there the surly village-churls,
And the red cloaks of market girls,
>   Pass onward from Shalott.

Sometimes a troop of damsels glad,
An abbot on an ambling pad,
Sometimes a curly shepherd-lad,
Or long-hair'd page in crimson clad,

Goes by to tower'd Camelot;
And sometimes thro' the mirror blue
The knights come riding two and two:
She hath no loyal knight and true,
   The Lady of Shalott.

But in her web she still delights
To weave the mirror's magic sights,
For often thro' the silent nights
A funeral, with plumes and lights,
   And music, went to Camelot:
Or when the moon was overhead,
Came two young lovers lately wed;
"I am half sick of shadows," said
   The Lady of Shalott.

Part III

A bow-shot from her bower-eaves,
He rode between the barley-sheaves,
The sun came dazzling thro' the leaves.
And flamed upon the brazen greaves
   Of bold Sir Lancelot.
A red-cross knight for ever kneel'd
To a lady in his shield,
That sparkled on the yellow field
   Beside remote Shalott.

The gemmy bridle glitter'd free,
Like to some branch of stars we see
Hung in the golden Galaxy.
The bridle bells rang merrily

    As he rode down to Camelot:
And from his blazon'd baldric slung
A mighty silver bugle hung,
And as he rode his armour rung,
    Beside remote Shalott.

All in the blue unclouded weather
Thick-jewell'd shone the saddle-leather,
The helmet and the helmet-feather
Burn'd like one burning flame together,
    As he rode down to Camelot.
As often thro' the purple night,
Below the starry clusters bright,
Some bearded meteor, trailing light,
    Moves over still Shalott.

His broad clear brow in sunlight glow'd;
On burnish'd hooves his war-horse trode;
From underneath his helmet flow'd
His coal-black curls as on he rode,
    As he rode down to Camelot.
From the bank and from the river
He flash'd into the crystal mirror,
" Tirra lirra," by the river
    Sang Sir Lancelot.

She left the web, she left the loom,
She made three paces thro' the room,
She saw the water-lily bloom,
She saw the helmet and the plume,

She look'd down to Camelot.
Out flew the web and floated wide;
The mirror crack'd from side to side
"The curse is come upon me," cried
    The Lady of Shalott.

Part IV

In the stormy east-wind straining,
The pale yellow woods were waning,
The broad stream in his banks complaining,
Heavily the low sky raining
    Over tower'd Camelot;
Down she came and found a boat
Beneath a willow left afloat,
And round about the prow she wrote
    The Lady of Shalott.

And down the river's dim expanse—
Like some bold sëer in a trance,
Seeing all his own mischance—
With a glassy countenance
    Did she look to Camelot.
And at the closing of the day
She loosed the chain, and down she lay;
The broad stream bore her far away,
    The Lady of Shalott.

Lying, robed in snowy white
That loosely flew to left and right—
The leaves upon her falling light—
Thro' the noises of the night

She floated down to Camelot:
And as the boat-head wound along
The willowy hills and fields among,
They heard her singing her last song,
　　　The Lady of Shalott.

Heard a carol, mournful, holy,
Chanted loudly, chanted lowly,
Till her blood was frozen slowly,
And her eyes were darken'd wholly,
　　　Turn'd to tower'd Camelot;
For ere she reach'd upon the tide
The first house by the water-side,
Singing in her song she died,
　　　The Lady of Shalott.

Under tower and balcony,
By garden-wall and gallery,
A gleaming shape she floated by,
Dead-pale between the houses high,
　　　Silent into Camelot.
Out upon the wharfs they came,
Knight and burgher, lord and dame,
And round the prow they read her name,
　　　The Lady of Shalott.

Who is this? and what is here?
And in the lighted palace near
Died the sound of royal cheer;
And they cross'd themselves for fear,

All the knights at Camelot:
But Lancelot mused a little space;
He said, ",She has a lovely face;
God in his mercy lend her grace,
    The Lady of Shalott.'

Alfred, Lord Tennyson.

Cornish Wind

THERE is a wind in Cornwall that I know
    From any other wind, because it smells
Of the warm honey breath of heather-bells
And of the sea's salt; and these meet and flow
With such sweet savour in such sharpness met
That the astonished sense in ecstasy
Tastes the ripe earth and the unvintaged sea.
Wind out of Cornwall, wind, if I forget:
Not in the tunnelled streets where scarce men breathe
The air they live by, but whatever seas
Blossom in foam, wherever merchant bees
Volubly traffic upon any heath :
If I forget, shame me ! or if I find
A wind in England like my Cornish wind.

Arthur Symons.

Lines from the "Milton" of
William Blake

THOU perceivest the Flowers put forth their precious Odours,
And none can tell how from so small a center comes such sweet,
Forgetting that within that Center Eternity expands
Its ever-during doors, that Og and Anak fiercely guard.
First, ere the morning breaks, joy opens in the flowery bosoms,
Joy even to tears, which the Sun rising dries; first the Wild Thyme
And Meadow-sweet, downy and soft, waving among the reeds,
Light springing in the air, lead the sweet Dance; they wake
The Honeysuckle sleeping on the Oak, the flaunting beauty
Revels along upon the wind; the White-thorn lovely May
Opens her many lovely eyes; listening, the Rose still sleeps.
None dare to wake her. Soon she bursts her crimson-curtained bed
And comes forth in the majesty of beauty; every Flower—
The Pink, the Jessamine, the Wallflower, the Carnation,

The Jonquil, the mild Lilly opes her heavens; every Tree
And Flower and Herb soon fill the air with an innumerable Dance,
Yet all in order sweet and lovely. . . .

Lines from " The Soul's Destroyer "

WE went together side by side to school,
    Together had our holidays in fields
Made golden by June's buttercups ; in woods,
Where under ferns fresh pulled I buried her,
And called her forth like Lazarus from the grave ;
She'd laughing come, to shake her curls until
Methought to hear full half a hundred bells.
A grown-up world took playful notice soon,
Made me feel shame that grew a greater love ;
She was more chary of her laughter then,
And more subdued her voice—as soft and sweet
As Autumn's, blowing through his golden reeds.
In her sweet sympathies she was a woman
When scarcely she was more than child in years,
And yet one angry moment parted us,
And days of longing never joined us more

William H. Davies.

Songs from "The Hollow Land"

I

QUEEN Mary's crown was gold,
King Joseph's crown was red,
But Jesus' crown was diamond
That lit up all the bed
     Mariae Virginis.

Ships sail through the heaven
With red banners dressed,
Carrying the planets seven
To see the white breast
     Mariae Virginis.

II

Christ keep the Hollow Land
Through the sweet springtide,
When the apple-blossoms bless
The lowly bent hillside.

Christ keep the Hollow Land
All the summer-tide ;
Still we cannot understand
Where the waters glide :
Only dimly seeing them
Coldly slipping through
Many green-lipped cavern mouths
Where the hills are blue.

William Morris.

From "Epipsychidion"

BUT the chief marvel of the wilderness
Is a lone dwelling, built by whom or how
None of the rustic island people know :
Tis not a tower of strength, though with its height
It overtops the woods ; but, for delight,
Some wise and tender Ocean-King, ere crime
Had been invented, in the world's young prime,
Reared it, a wonder of that simple time,
An envy of the isles, a pleasure-house
Made sacred to his sister and his spouse.
It scarce seems now a wreck of human art,
But, as it were Titanic ; in the heart
Of Earth having assumed its form, then grown
Out of the mountains, from the living stone,
Lifting itself in caverns light and high :
For all the antique and learnèd imagery
Has been erased, and in the place of it
The ivy and the wild-vine interknit
The volumes of their many-twining stems:
Parasite flowers illume with dewy gems
The lampless halls, and when they fade, the sky
Peeps through their winter-woof of tracery
With moonlight patches, or star atoms keen,
Or fragments of the day's intense serene ;—
Working mosaic on their Parian floors.
And, day and night, aloof, from the high towers
And terraces, the Earth and Ocean seem
To sleep in one another's arms, and dream

Of waves, flowers, clouds, woods, rocks, and all
    that we
Read in their smiles and call reality.

  This isle and house are mine, and I have vowed
Thee to be lady of the solitude.—
And I have fitted up some chambers there
Looking towards the golden Eastern air,
And level with the living winds, which flow
Like waves above the living waves below.—
I have sent books and music there, and all
Those instruments with which high Spirits call
The future from its cradle, and the past
Out of its grave, and make the present last
In thoughts and joys which sleep, but cannot die,
Folded within their own eternity.
Our simple life wants little, and true taste
Hires not the pale drudge Luxury, to waste
The scene it would adorn and therefore still,
Nature with all her children haunts the hill.
The ring-dove, in the embowering ivy, yet
Keeps up her love-lament, and the owls flit
Round the evening tower, and the young stars
    glance
Between the quick bats in their twilight dance;
The spotted deer bask in the fresh moonlight
Before our gate, and the slow, silent night
Is measured by the pants of their calm sleep.
Be this our home in life, and when years heap
Their withered hours, like leaves, on our decay,
Let us become the overhanging day,

The living soul of this Elysian isle,
Conscious, inseparable, one. Meanwhile
We two will rise, and sit, and walk together,
Under the roof of blue Ionian weather,
And wander in the meadows, or ascend
The mossy mountains, where the blue heavens bend
With lightest winds, to touch their paramour ;
Or linger, where the pebble-paven shore,
Under the quick, faint kisses of the sea
Trembles and sparkles as with ecstasy,—
Possessing and possessed by all that is
Within that calm circumference of bliss,
And by each other, till to love and live
Be one :—or, at the noontide hour, arrive
Where some old cavern hoar seems yet to keep
The moonlight of the expired night asleep,
Through which the awakened day can never peep;
A veil for our seclusion, close as night's,
Where secure sleep may kill thine innocent lights ;
Sleep, the fresh dew of languid love, the rain
Whose drops quench kisses till they burn again.
And we will talk, until thought's melody
Become too sweet for utterance, and it die
In words, to live again in looks, which dart
With thrilling tone into the voiceless heart,
Harmonising silence without a sound.
Our breath shall intermix, our bosoms bound,
And our veins beat together ; and our lips
With other eloquence than words, eclipse
The soul that burns between them, and the wells
Which boil under our being's inmost cells,

The fountains of our deepest life, shall be
Confused in Passion's golden purity,
As mountain-springs under the morning sun.
We shall become the same, we shall be one
Spirit within two frames, oh! wherefore two?
One passion in twin-hearts, which grows and grew,
Till like two meteors of expanding flame,
Those spheres instinct with it become the same,
Touch, mingle, are transfigured; ever still
Burning, yet ever inconsumable;
In one another's substance finding food,
Like flames too pure and light and unimbued
To nourish their bright lives with baser prey,
Which point to Heaven and cannot pass away.
One hope within two wills, one will beneath
Two overshadowing minds, one life, one death,
One Heaven, one Hell, one immortality,
And one annihilation. Woe is me!
The wingèd words on which my soul would pierce
Into the height of Love's rare Universe,
Are chains of lead around its flight of fire—
I pant, I sink, I tremble, I expire!

Percy Bysshe Shelley.

Malvolio ∾ ∾ ∾

THOU hast been very tender to the moon,
   Malvolio! and on many a daffodil
And many a daisy hast thou yearn'd, until
The nether jaw quiver'd with thy good heart.

But tell me now, Malvolio, tell me true,
Hast thou not sometimes driven from their play
The village children, when they came too near
Thy study, if hit ball rais'd shouts around,
Or if delusive trap shook off thy muse,
Pregnant with wonders for another age?
Hast thou sat still and patient (tho' sore prest
Hearthward to stoop and warm thy blue-nail'd hand)
Lest thou shouldst frighten from a frosty fare
The speckled thrush, raising his bill aloft
To swallow the red berry on the ash
By thy white window, three short paces off?
If *this* thou hast not done, and hast done *that*,
I do exile thee from the moon twelve whole
Calendar months, debarring thee from use
Of rose, bud, blossom, odour, simile,
And furthermore I do hereby pronounce
Divorce between the nightingale and thee.
Walter Savage Landor.

Daffadill

THROUGH yonder vale as I did pass,
   Descending from the hill,
I met a smirking bonny lass;
   They call her Daffadill.

Whose presence as along she went
   The pretty flowers did greet
As though their heads they downward bent
   With homage to her feet.

And all the shepherds that were nigh
From top of every hill
Unto the valleys loud did cry
"There goes sweet Daffadill."
Michael Drayton.

The Dream Garden

WITH that my hond in his he took anoon,
   Of which I comfort caughte, and went in faste;
But Lord! so I was glad and wel begoon!
For overal wher that I myn eyén caste
Were treës clad with leves that ay shal laste,
Eche in his kynde, of colour fresch and grene
As emeraude, that joye it was to sene.

The bildere ook and eek the hardy asshe;
The piler elm, the cofre unto careyne;
The boxtree piper; holm to whippés lasshe;
The saylyng firr; the cipres, deth to pleyne;
The sheter ew; the asp for shaftës pleyne;
The olyve of pees, and eek the drunken vyne;
The victor palm, the laurer to devyne.

A garden saw I ful of blosmy bowés
Upon a river in a grené mede,
There as ther swetnesse evermore y-now is;
With flourés whité, blewé, yelwe, and rede,
And coldé wellé-stremés, nothyng dede,
That swommen ful of smalé fischés lighte,
With fynnés rede and scalés silver-brighte.

On every bough the briddés herde I synge,
With voys of aungel in her armonye ;
Som besyede hem hir briddés forth to brynge.
The litel conyes to hir pley gunne hye ;
And further al aboute I gan aspye
The dredful roo, the buk, the hert, and hynde,
Squerels and bestés smale of gentil kynde.

Of instruments of strengés in acord
Herde I so pleye a ravisshyng swetnesse,
That God, that maker is of al and Lord,
Ne herdé never beter, as I gesse ;
Therewith a wynd, unnethe it myghte be lesse,
Made in the levés grene a noysé softe,
Accordant to the foule's songe on-lofte.

The air of that place so attempré was
That never was grevaunce of hoot ne cold ;
There wex eek every holsom spice and gras ;
Ne no man may ther wexé seek ne old,
Yit was ther joyé more a thousand fold
Than man can telle ; ne never wolde it nyghte,
But ay cleer day to any manne's sighte.

Geoffrey Chaucer.

Lines to a Dragon-Fly

LIFE (priest and poet say) is but a dream ;
  I wish no happier one than to be laid
    Beneath a cool syringa's scented shade,
Or wavy willow, by the running stream,

    Brimful of moral, where the dragon-fly
      Wanders as careless and content as I.
Thanks for this fancy, insect king,
Of purple crest and filmy wing,
Who with indifference givest up
The water-lily's golden cup,
To come again and overlook
What I am writing in my book.
Believe me, most who read the line
Will read with hornier eyes than thine ;
And yet their souls shall live for ever,
And thine drop dead into the river !
God pardon them, O insect king,
Who fancy so unjust a thing !

                        Walter Savage Landor.

To John Poins

I COULD never yet
   Hang on their sleeves that weigh, as thou may'st see,
A chip of chance more than a pound of wit :
This maketh me at home to hunt and hawk ;
And in foul weather at my book to sit ;
In frost and snow, then with my bow to stalk :
No man doth mark whereso I ride or go :
In lusty leas at liberty I walk ;
And of these news I feel nor weal nor woe ;
Save that a clog doth hang yet at my heel.
No force for that, for it is order'd so

That I may leap both hedge and dyke full well.
I am not now in France, to judge the wine;
With savoury sauce those delicates to feel:
Nor yet in Spain, where one must him incline
Rather than to be, outwardly to seem.
I meddle not with wits that be so fine;
Nor Flanders' cheer lets not my sight to deem
Of black and white; nor takes my wits away
With beastliness; such do those beasts esteem
Nor I am not, where truth is given in prey
For money, poison and treason; of some
A common practice, used night and day.
But I am here in Kent and Christendom,
Among the Muses, where I read and rhyme;
Where if thou list, mine own John Poins, to come,
Thou shalt be judge how I do spend my time.
Sir Thomas Wyatt.

To the Cuckoo

HAIL, beauteous stranger of the grove!
  Thou messenger of Spring!
Now Heaven repairs thy rural seat,
  And woods thy welcome sing.

What time the daisy decks the green,
  Thy certain voice we hear;
Hast thou a star to guide thy path,
  Or mark the rolling year?

Delightful visitant! with thee
  I hail the time of flowers,
And hear the sound of music sweet
  From birds among the bowers.

The school-boy, wandering through the wood
  To pull the primrose gay,
Starts, the new voice of Spring to hear,
  And imitates thy lay.

What time the pea puts on the bloom,
  Thou fliest thy vocal vale,
An annual guest in other lands,
  Another Spring to hail.

Sweet bird! thy bower is ever green,
  Thy sky is ever clear,
Thou hast no sorrow in thy song,
  No Winter in thy year!

Oh, could I fly, I'd fly with thee!
  We'd make, with joyful wing,
Our annual visit o'er the globe,
  Companions of the Spring.

John Logan.

The Question

I DREAMED that, as I wandered by the way,
  Bare Winter suddenly was changed to Spring
And gentle odours led my steps astray,
  Mixed with a sound of waters murmuring
Along a shelving bank of turf, which lay
  Under a copse, and hardly dared to fling

Its green arms round the bosom of the stream,
But kissed it and then fled, as thou mightest in
 dream.

There grew pied wind-flowers and violets,
  Daisies, those pearled Arcturi of the earth,
The constellated flower that never sets ;
  Faint oxlips; tender bluebells, at whose birth
The sod scarce heaved ; and that tall flower that
  wets—
  Like a child, half in tenderness and mirth—
Its mother's face with Heaven's collected tears,
When the low wind, its playmate's voice, it hears.

And in the warm hedge grew lush eglantine,
  Green cowbind and the moonlight-coloured may,
And cherry-blossoms, and white cups, whose wine
  Was the bright dew, yet drained not by the day;
And wild roses, and ivy serpentine,
  With its dark buds and leaves, wandering astray;
And flowers azure, black, and streaked with gold,
Fairer than any wakened eyes behold.

And nearer to the river's trembling edge
  There grew broad flag flowers, purple pranked
    with white,
And starry river buds among the sedge,
  And floating water-lilies, broad and bright,
Which lit the oak that overhung the hedge
  With moonlight beams of their own watery light;
And bulrushes, and reeds of such deep green
As soothed the dazzled eyes with sober sheen.

Methought that of these visionary flowers
   I made a nosegay, bound in such a way
That the same hues, which in their natural bowers
   Were mingled or opposed, the like array
Kept these imprisoned children of the Hours
   Within my hand,—and then, elate and gay,
I hastened to the spot whence I had come,
That I might there present it!—Oh! to whom?

Percy Bysshe Shelley.

To the River Duddon: Farewell

I THOUGHT of Thee, my partner and my guide,
   As being pass'd away. Vain sympathies!
   For backward, Duddon! as I cast my eyes,
I see what was, and is, and will abide;
Still glides the Stream, and shall for ever glide;
   The Form remains, the Function never dies;
   While we, the brave, the mighty, and the wise,
We Men, who in our morn of youth defied
The elements, must vanish;—be it so!
   Enough, if something from our hands have power
   To live, and act, and serve the future hour;
And if, as toward the silent tomb we go,
   Through love, through hope, and faith's transcendent dower,
We feel that we are greater than we know.

William Wordsworth.

Yew Trees

THERE is a Yew-tree, pride of Lorton Vale,
Which to this day stands single, in the midst
Of its own darkness, as it stood of yore;
Not loth to furnish weapons for the bands
Of Umfraville or Percy ere they marched
To Scotland's heaths; or those that crossed the sea
And drew their sounding bows at Azincour,
Perhaps at earlier Cressy, or Poictiers.
Of vast circumference and gloom profound
This solitary Tree! a living thing
Produced too slowly ever to decay;
Of form and aspect too magnificent
To be destroyed. But worthier still of note
Are those fraternal Four of Borrowdale,
Joined in one solemn and capacious grove;
Huge trunks! and each particular trunk a growth
Of intertwisted fibres serpentine
Up-coiling, and inveterately convolved;
Nor uninformed with Phantasy, and looks
That threaten the profane; a pillared shade,
Upon whose grassless floor of red-brown hue,
By sheddings from the pining umbrage tinged
Perennially—beneath whose sable roof
Of boughs as if for festal purpose decked
With unrejoicing berries—ghostly Shapes
May meet at noontide; Fear and trembling Hope,
Silence and Foresight; Death the Skeleton
And Time the Shadow;—there to celebrate,
As in a natural temple scattered o'er

With altars undisturbed of mossy stone,
United worship ; or in mute repose
To lie, and listen to the mountain flood
Murmuring from Glaramara's inmost caves.
William Wordsworth.

A Sea Change

THIS song the sea sings strikes the inner ear
   O'erlaid and deafened by the city's din,
  The odours of the sea and down let in
Lost thoughts of many an ancient hope and fear:
The wind blows through me, carrying clean away
   The dust that long has settled on my heart—
  The flying motes blown in from street and mart
And all the idle business of the day—
The second self—all men's by fate or choice—
   Drops from me like a garment : I am one
  With those wild sons of Earth whose race was
     run,
   Long ages ere she brought forth men like me.
And so she hails me, with a mother's voice,
  A primal man beside a primal sea.
Walter Hogg.

Nutting

IT seems a day
  (I speak of one from many singled out)
One of those heavenly days that cannot die ;
When, in the eagerness of boyish hope,

I left our cottage-threshold, sallying forth
With a huge wallet o'er my shoulders slung,
A nutting-crook in hand ; and turned my steps
Toward some far-distant wood, a Figure quaint,
Tricked out in proud disguise of cast-off weeds
Which for that service had been husbanded,
By exhortation of my frugal Dame—
Motley accoutrement. of power to smile
At thorns, and brakes, and brambles,—and in truth
More ragged than need was ! O'er pathless rocks,
Through beds of matted fern, and tangled thickets,
Forcing my way, I came to one dear nook
Unvisited, where not a broken bough
Drooped with its withered leaves, ungracious sign
Of devastation ; but the hazels rose
Tall and erect, with tempting clusters hung,
A virgin scene :—A little while I stood,
Breathing with such suppression of the heart
As joy delights in ; and with wise restraint
Voluptuous, fearless of a rival, eyed
The banquet ;—or beneath the trees I sate
Among the flowers, and with the flowers I played ;
A temper known to those who, after long
And weary expectation, have been blest
With sudden happiness beyond all hope.
Perhaps it was a bower beneath whose leaves
The violets of five seasons re-appear
And fade, unseen by any human eye ;
Where fairy water-breaks do murmur on
For ever ; and I saw the sparkling foam,
And—with my cheek on one of those green stones

That, fleeced with moss, under the shady trees
Lay round me, scattered like a flock of sheep—
I heard the murmur and the murmuring sound,
In that sweet mood when pleasure loves to pay
Tribute to ease ; and, of its joy secure,
The heart luxuriates with indifferent things,
Wasting its kindliness on stocks and stones,
And on the vacant air.   Then up I rose,
And dragged to earth both branch and bough, with crash
And merciless ravage : and the shady nook
Of hazels, and the green and mossy bower,
Deformed and sullied, patiently gave up
Their quiet being : and unless I now
Confound my present feelings with the past,
Ere from the mutilated bower I turned
Exulting, rich beyond the wealth of kings,
I felt a sense of pain when I beheld
The silent trees, and saw the intruding sky.—
Then, dearest Maiden, move along these shades
In gentleness of heart ; with gentle hand
Touch—for there is a spirit in the woods.

William Wordsworth.

Under the Lime Tree

UNDER the lime-tree on the daisied ground,
   Two that I know of made their bed :
There you may see, heaped and scattered round,
   Grass and blossoms, broken and shed,

All in a thicket down in a dale;
        Tandaradei—
Sweetly sang the nightingale.

Ere I set foot in the meadow, already
  Some one was waiting for somebody;
There was a meeting—O gracious lady!
  There is no pleasure again for me.
Thousands of kisses there he took,—
        Tandaradei—
See my lips, how red they look!

Leaf and blossom he had pulled and piled
  For a couch, a green one, soft and high;
And many a one hath gazed and smiled,
  Passing the bower and pressed grass by;
And the roses crushed hath seen,—
        Tandaradei—
Where I laid my head between.

In this love passage, if any one had been there,
  How sad and shamed should I be!
But what were we a-doing alone among the green
      there,
  No soul shall ever know except my love and me,
And the little nightingale.—
        Tandaradei—
She, I think, will tell no tale.

            [Translated from the German by
                Thomas Lovell Beddoes.

Populous Solitude   ∽   ∽   ∽

WHEN we were idlers with the loitering rills,
   The need of human love we little noted:
     Our love was nature; and the peace that floated
On the white mist, and dwelt upon the hills,
To sweet accord subdued our wayward wills:
   One soul was ours, one mind, one heart devoted,
   That, wisely doting, ask'd not why it doted,
And ours the unknown joy, which knowing kills.
But now I find how dear thou wert to me;
   That man is more than half of nature's treasure,
Of that fair beauty which no eye can see,
   Of that sweet music which no ear can measure;
   And now the streams may sing for others' pleasure,
The hills sleep on in their eternity.

                          Hartley Coleridge.

A Solitude within a Solitude   ∽   ∽

THE irresponsive silence of the land,
   The irresponsive sounding of the sea,
     Speak both one message of one sense to me:—
Aloof, aloof, we stand aloof, so stand
Thou too aloof, bound with the flawless band
   Of inner solitude; we bind not thee;
   But who from thy self-chain shall set thee free?
What heart shall touch thy heart? What hand thy
       hand?
And I am sometimes proud and sometimes meek,

And sometimes I remember days of old
When fellowship seem'd not so far to seek,
    And all the world and I seem'd much less cold,
    And at the rainbow's foot lay surely gold,
And hope felt strong, and life itself not weak.

Christina Rossetti.

Tweed and Till

SAYS Tweed to Till—
  "What gars ye rin sae still?"
Says Till to Tweed—
  "Though ye rin with speed
    And I rin slaw,
For ae man that ye droon
  I droon twa."

Anonymous.

A Runnable Stag

WHEN the pods went pop on the broom, green broom,
  And apples began to be golden-skinned,
We harboured a stag in the Priory coomb,
  And we feathered his trail up-wind, up-wind,
  We feathered his trail up-wind—
    A stag of warrant, a stag, a stag,
    A runnable stag, a kingly crop,
    Brow, bay and tray and three on top,
    A stag, a runnable stag.

Then the huntsman's horn rang yap, yap, yap,
   And "Forwards" we heard the harbourer shout;
But 'twas only a brocket that broke a gap
   In the beechen underwood, driven out,
   From the underwood antlered out
     By warrant and might of the stag, the stag,
     The runnable stag, whose lordly mind
     Was bent on sleep, though beamed and tined
     He stood, a runnable stag.

So we tufted the covert till afternoon
   With Tinkerman's Pup and Bell-of-the-North;
And hunters were sulky and hounds out of tune
   Before we tufted the right stag forth,
   Before we tufted him forth,
     The stag of warrant, the wily stag,
     The runnable stag with his kingly crop,
     Brow, bay and tray and three on top,
     The royal and runnable stag.

It was Bell-of-the-North and Tinkerman's Pup
   That stuck to the scent till the copse was drawn.
"Tally ho! tally ho!" and the hunt was up,
   The tufters whipped and the pack laid on,
   The resolute pack laid on,
     And the stag of warrant away at last,
     The runnable stag, the same, the same,
     His hoofs on fire, his horns like flame,
     A stag, a runnable stag.

"Let your gelding be: if you check or chide
   He stumbles at once and you're out of the hunt;
For three hundred gentlemen, able to ride,
   On hunters accustomed to bear the brunt,
   Accustomed to bear the brunt,
     Are after the runnable stag, the stag,
     The runnable stag with his kingly crop,
     Brow, bay and tray and three on top,
     The right, the runnable stag."

By perilous paths in coomb and dell,
   The heather, the rocks, and the river-bed,
The pace grew hot, for the scent lay well,
   And a runnable stag goes right ahead,
   The quarry went right ahead—
     Ahead, ahead, and fast and far;
     His antlered crest, his cloven hoof,
     Brow, bay and tray and three aloof,
     The stag, the runnable stag.

For a matter of twenty miles and more,
   By the densest hedge and the highest wall,
Through herds of bullocks he baffled the lore
   Of harbourer, huntsmen, hounds and all,
   Of harbourer, hounds and all—
     The stag of warrant, the wily stag,
     For twenty miles, and five and five,
     He ran, and he never was caught alive,
     This stag, this runnable stag.

When he turned at bay in the leafy gloom,
   In the emerald gloom where the brook ran deep,
He heard in the distance the rollers boom,
   And he saw in a vision of peaceful sleep,
   In a wonderful vision of sleep,
     A stag of warrant, a stag, a stag,
     A runnable stag in a jewelled bed,
     Under the sheltering ocean dead,
     A stag, a runnable stag.

So a fateful hope lit up his eye,
   And he opened his nostrils wide again,
And he tossed his branching antlers high
   As he headed the hunt down Charlock glen,
   As he raced down the echoing glen
     For five miles more, the stag, the stag,
     For twenty miles, and five and five,
     Not to be caught now, dead or alive,
     The stag, the runnable stag.

Three hundred gentlemen, able to ride,
   Three hundred horses as gallant and free,
Beheld him escape on the evening tide,
   Far out till he sank in the Severn Sea,
   Till he sank in the depths of the sea—
     The stag, the buoyant stag, the stag
     That slept at last in a jewelled bed
     Under the sheltering ocean spread,
     The stag, the runnable stag.

                        John Davidson.

The Dairymaids to Pan

GOATFOOT, we know you,
　　Though we cannot see you;
Goatfoot, Goatfoot,
Lightfoot, do we flee you.
When we hear the flocks at night
Bleat as to the shepherd's light
Then we girls clasp close in bed,
Draw the coarse sheet overhead,
Whispering, afraid to sleep,
"'Tis the good God Goatfoot
Fondling the sheep."

Goatfoot, we hear you
At the cow-house door,
Goatfoot, Goatfoot,
Through a single floor.
Barefoot in our nightgowns then
Timidly we wake the men:
To the byre they venture slowly—
As each happy cow lows lowly
Each hind in his turn repeats
"'Tis the good God Goatfoot
Easing their teats."

Goatfoot, do not fright us
In the woodland meadows.
Goatfoot, Goatfoot,
When the kine have led us
Far from home at milking-time
Down dark groves of scented lime

1o the weedy water where
Deep they wade for cooler air.
Think of all your fruited feasts;
Be the good God Goatfoot
To herd us our beasts.

Gordon Bottomley.

The Birth of Robin Hood

O WILLIE'S large o' limb and lith,
    And come o' high degree;
And he is gone to Earl Richard
    To serve for meat and fee.

Earl Richard had but ae daughter,
    Fair as a lily flower;
And they made up their love-contract
    Like proper paramour.

It fell upon a simmers nicht
    Whan the leaves were fair and green,
That Willie met his gay ladie
    Intil the wood alane.

"O narrow is my gown, Willie,
    That wont to be sae wide,
And gane is a' my fair colour,
    That wont to be my pride.

"But gin my father should get word
    What's past between us twa,
Before that he should eat or drink,
    He'd hang you o'er that wa'.

"But ye'll come to my bower, Willie,
　At the setting of the sun ;
And kep me in your arms twa,
　And letna me fa' down."

O whan the sun was near gane down,
　He's doen him till her bower ;
And there, by the lee licht o' the moon,
　Her window she lookit o'er.

Intill a robe o' red scarlet
　She lap, and caught nae harm ;
Willie was large o' lith and limb,
　And keepit her in his arm.

And they've gane to the good greenwood,
　And ere the night was dune,
She's borne to him a bonny young son,
　Amang the leaves sae green.

When night was gane and day was come,
　And the sun began to peep,
Up and rose the Earl Richard
　Out o' his drowsy sleep.

He's ca'd upon his merry young men,
　By ane, by twa, and by three,
"O what's come o' my daughter dear,
　That she's na come to me?

"I dreamt a dreary dream last night—
　God grant it come to guid !
I dreamt I saw my daughter dear
　Drown in the saut sea flood.

"My daughter, maybe, is dead or sick;
  Or gin she be stown awa',
I mak' a vow, and I'll keep it true,
  I'll hang ye ane and a'!"

They sought her back, they sought her fore,
  They sought her up and down;
They got her in the guid greenwood
  Nursing her bonny young son.

He took the bonny boy in his arms,
  And kist him tenderlie;
Says, "Though I would your father hang,
  Your mother's dear to me."

He kist him o'er and o'er again;
  "My grandson I thee claim;
And Robin Hood in guid greenwood,
  'Tis that shall be your name."

There's mony ane sings o' grass, o' grass,
  And mony ane sings o' corn;
And mony ane sings o' Robin Hood,
  Kens little whar' he was born.

It was na in the ha', the ha',
  Nor in the painted bower;
But it was in the guid greenwood,
  Amang the lily flower.

Anonymous.

The Bold Pedlar and Robin Hood

THERE chanced to be a pedlar bold,
   A pedlar bold he chanced to be;
He rolled his pack all on his back,
   And he came tripping o'er the lee—
     Down a down a down a down,
      Down a down a down.

By chance he met two troublesome blades,
   Two troublesome blades they chanced to be;
The one of them was bold Robin Hood,
   And the other was Little John so free.

"O pedlar, pedlar, what is in thy pack?
   Come speedily and tell to me":
"I've several suits of the gay green silks,
   And silken bow-strings two or three."

"If you have several suits of the gay green silk,
   And silken bow-strings two or three,
Then it's by my body," cries Little John,
   "One half your pack shall belong to me."

"O nay, O nay," says the pedlar bold,
   "O nay, O nay, that never can be;
For there's never a man from fair Nottingham
   Can take one half my pack from me."

Then the pedlar he pulled off his pack,
   And put it a little below his knee,
Saying, "If you do move me one perch from this,
   My pack and all shall gang with thee."

Then Little John he drew his sword,
   The pedlar by his pack did stand;
They fought until they both did sweat,
   Till he cried, "Pedlar, pray hold your hand!

Then Robin Hood he was standing by,
   And he did laugh most heartilie;
Saying, "I could find a man, of a smaller scale,
   Could thrash the pedlar and also thee."

"Go you try, master," says Little John,
   "Go you try, master, most speedily,
Or by my body," says Little John,
   "I am sure this night you will not know me."

Then Robin Hood he drew his sword,
   And the pedlar by his pack did stand;
They fought till the blood in streams did flow,
   Till he cried, "Pedlar, pray hold your hand!'

"Pedlar, Pedlar, what is thy name?
   Come speedily and tell to me."
"My name! my name I ne'er will tell
   Till both your names you have told to me."

"The one of us is bold Robin Hood,
   And the other Little John so free";
"Now," says the pedlar, "it lays to my good will,
   Whether my name I choose to tell to thee.

"I am Gamble Gold of the gay greenwoods,
   And travelled far beyond the sea;
For killing a man in my father's land
   From my country I was forced to flee."

"If you are Gamble Gold of the gay greenwoods,
  And travelled far beyond the sea,
You are my mother's own sister's son;
  What nearer cousins then can we be?"

They sheathed their swords with friendly words,
  So merrily they did agree;
They went to a tavern, and there they dined,
  And bottles cracked most merrily.

Anonymous.

Robin Hood's Funeral

WEEP, weep, ye woodmen! wail;
  Your hands with sorrow wring!
Your master Robin Hood lies dead,
  Therefore sigh as you sing.

Here lie his primer and his beads,
  His bent bow and his arrows keen,
His good sword and his holy cross:
  Now cast on flowers fresh and green.

And, as they fall, shed tears and say
  Well, well-a-day! well, well-a-day!
Thus cast ye flowers fresh, and sing,
  And on to Wakefield take your way.

Anthony Munday.

Full Summer

WHENAS the rye reach to the chin,
  And chopcherry, chopcherry ripe within,
Strawberries swimming in the cream,
And schoolboys playing in the stream;
Then, O, then, O, then, O, my true love said,
'Till that time come again
She could not live a maid.

George Peele

Meg Merrilies

OLD Meg she was a gipsy;
  And lived upon the moors:
Her bed it was the brown heath turf,
  And her house was out of doors.
Her apples were swart blackberries,
  Her currants, pods o' broom;
Her wine was dew of the wild white rose,
  Her book a churchyard tomb.

Her brothers were the craggy hills,
  Her sisters larchen trees;
Alone with her great family
  She lived as she did please.
No breakfast had she many a morn,
  No dinner many a noon,
And, 'stead of supper, she would stare
  Full hard against the moon.

But every morn, of woodbine fresh
   She made her garlanding,
And, every night, the dark glen yew
   She wove, and she would sing.
And with her fingers, old and brown,
   She plaited mats of rushes,
And gave them to the cottagers
   She met among the bushes.

Old Meg was brave as Margaret Queen,
   And tall as Amazon ;
An old red blanket cloak she wore,
   A chip-hat had she on :
God rest her aged bones somewhere !
   She died full long agone.

John Keats.

Un Roseau Pensant

PAN'S Syrinx was a girl indeed,
   Though now she's turned into a reed ;
From that dear reed Pan's pipe does come,
A pipe that strikes Apollo dumb ;
Nor flute, nor lute, nor gittern can
So chant it as the pipe of Pan :
Cross-gartered swains and dairy girls,
With faces smug and round as pearls,
When Pan's shrill pipe begins to play,
With dancing wear out night and day ;

The bagpipe's drone his hum lays by,
When Pan sounds up his minstrelsy;
His minstrelsy! O base! this quill,
Which at my mouth with wind I fill,
Puts me in mind, though her I miss,
That still my Syrinx' lips I kiss.

John Lyly.

Sir Lancelot and Queen Guinevere

LIKE souls that balance joy and pain,
With tears and smiles from heaven again
The maiden spring upon the plain
Came in a sun-lit fall of rain.
    In crystal vapour everywhere
Blue isles of heaven laugh'd between,
And, far in forest-deeps unseen,
The topmost elm-tree gather'd green
    From draughts of balmy air.

Sometimes the linnet piped his song:
Sometimes the throstle whistled strong:
Sometimes the sparhawk, wheel'd along,
Hush'd all the groves from fear of wrong:
    By grassy capes with fuller sound
In curves the yellowing river ran,
And drooping chestnut-buds began
To spread into the perfect fan,
    Above the teeming ground.

Then, in the boyhood of the year
Sir Lancelot and Queen Guinevere
Rode thro' the coverts of the deer,
With blissful treble ringing clear.
    She seemed a part of joyous Spring:
A gown of grass-green silk she wore,
Buckled with golden clasps before;
A light-green tuft of plumes she bore
    Closed in a golden ring.

Now on some twisted ivy-net,
Now by some tinkling rivulet,
In mosses mixt with violet
Her cream-white mule his pastern set:
    And fleeter now she skimm'd the plains
Than she whose elfin prancer springs
By night to eery warblings,
When all the glimmering moorland rings
    With jingling bridle-reins.

As she fled fast thro' sun and shade.
The happy winds upon her play'd,
Blowing the ringlet from the braid:
She look'd so lovely, as she sway'd
    The rein with dainty finger tips,
A man had given all other bliss,
And all his worldly worth for this,
To waste his whole heart in one kiss
    Upon her perfect lips.

Lord Tennyson.

The Moods

TIME drops in decay,
   Like a candle burnt out,
And the mountains and woods
Have their day, have their day ;
What one in the rout
Of the fire-born moods
Has fallen away?   *W. B. Yeats.*

Song

SHAKE off your heavy trance !
   And leap into a dance
Such as no mortals used to tread :
   Fit only for Apollo
To play to, for the moon to lead,
   And all the stars to follow !

Francis Beaumont

The Angler's Song

Man's life is but vain, for 'tis sub-ject to pain And sor-row, and short as a bub-ble; 'Tis a hodgpodg of

businesse, and money and care, And care and money, and trouble.

But we'll take no care, when the weather prove fair, Nor

will we vex now though it rain; We'll ban-ish all sor-row and

sing till to-mor-row, And an-gle and an-gle a-gain.

As I Walked Forth   ∽   ∽   ∽

As I walked forth one sum-mer's day,

To view the mea - dows green and gay,

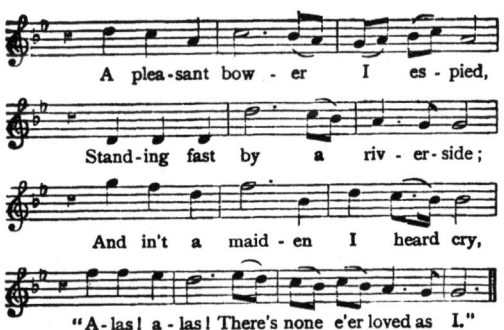

A pleasant bower I espied,
Standing fast by a riverside;
And in't a maiden I heard cry,
"Alas! alas! There's none e'er loved as I."

II

Then round the Meadow did she walk,
Gathering each flower by the stalk;
Such flowers as in the meadow grew,
The Dead Man's Thumb, an herb all blue;
And as she pulled them still cryed she
Alas! Alas! None ever loved like me!

III

When she had filled her Apron full
Of such green things as she could cull,
The green leaves served her for a Bed,
The flowers were Pillow for her Head:
Then down she laid, ne'er more did speak,
Alas! Alas! with Love her heart did break.

Dabbling in the Dew

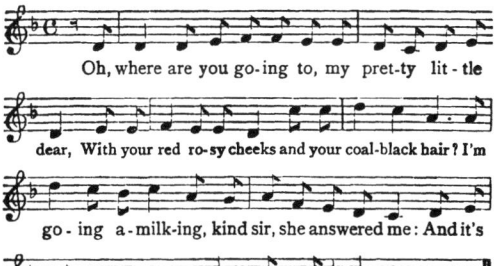

From "Folk Songs from Somerset." Edited by Cecil Sharp and Charles L. Marson

Oh, where are you go-ing to, my pret-ty lit-tle dear, With your red ro-sy cheeks and your coal-black hair? I'm go-ing a-milk-ing, kind sir, she answered me: And it's dabbling in the dew makes the milk-maids fair.

II

Suppose I were to clothe you, my pretty little dear,
In a green silken gown and the amethyst rare?
O no, sir, O no, sir, kind sir, she answered me,
For it's dabbling in the dew makes the milkmaids fair!

III

Suppose I were to carry you, my pretty little dear,
In a chariot with horses, a grey gallant pair?
O no, sir, O no, sir, kind sir, she answered me,
For it's dabbling in the dew makes the milkmaids fair!

IV

Suppose I were to feast you, my pretty little dear,
With dainties on silver, the whole of the year?

O no, sir, O no, sir, kind sir, she answered me,
For it's dabbling in the dew makes the milkmaids fair!

V

O but London's a city, my pretty little dear,
And all men are gallant and brave that are there—
O no, sir, O no, sir, kind sir, she answered me,
For it's dabbling in the dew makes the milkmaids fair!

VI

O fine clothes and dainties and carriages so rare
Bring grey to the cheeks and silver to the hair;
What's a ring on the finger if rings are round the eye?
But it's dabbling in the dew makes the milkmaids fair!

Sweet Primeroses

Westmorland

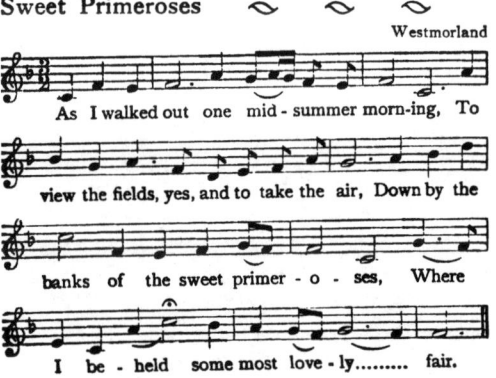

As I walked out one mid-summer morning, To view the fields, yes, and to take the air, Down by the banks of the sweet primer-o-ses, Where I beheld some most love-ly......... fair.

II

It's three long steps I took up to her,
Thinking to keep her by my side;
Which, when I closer came to view her,
She appeared to me like some virtuous bride.

III

I said "Fair maid, where are you going,
Or what is the cause of all your grief,
I'll make you as happy as any lady
If you will grant to me one small relief."

IV

"Stand off, stand off, you are deceitful,
You are a false and deceitful man,
For it's you that have caused my poor heart to wander,
And for to give me relief that's all in vain.

V

"I'm going down to some lonesome valley
Where neither man nor mortal shall me find,
Where those pretty little small birds are changing their voices,
And at every moment blows blustering wind.

VI

"Come all ye fair maids that go a courting,
Take warning by what I'm going to say,
For young men are like a star on a summer's morning,
When daylight does appear they fade away."

A-begging we will go

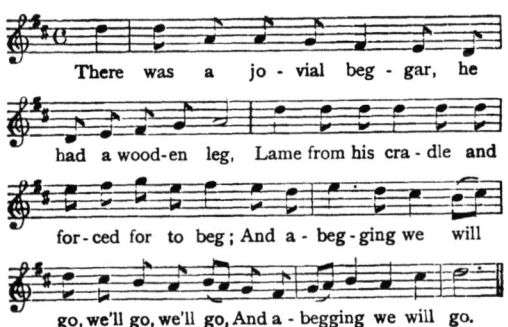

There was a jo-vial beg-gar, he had a wood-en leg, Lame from his cra-dle and for-ced for to beg; And a-beg-ging we will go, we'll go, we'll go, And a-begging we will go.

II

A bag for his Oatmeal
Another for his Salt,
And a pair of Crutches
To show that he can halt,
    And a-begging we will go.

III

A bag for his Wheat,
Another for his Rye,
A little bottle by his side
To drink when he's a-dry,
    And a-begging we will go.

IV

To Pimblico we'll go,
Where we shall Merry be,
With every Man a can in's Hand
And a Wench upon his Knee.
    And a-begging we will go.

(One verse omitted here.)

V

Of all occupations
A Begger lives the best,
For when he is a-weary
He'll lie him down and rest.
    And a-begging we will go.

VI

I fear no Plots against me.
I live in open Cell ;
Then who would be a King,
When the Beggers live so well?
    And a-begging we will go.

lov - ed you so long, De - light - ing in your com - pa - ny. Green - sleeves was all my joy, Green - sleeves was my de-light, Green-sleeves was my heart of gold, And who but La-die Green-sleeves?

II

I have been ready at your hand
  To grant whatever you would crave,
I have both waged life and land
  Your love and good will for to have.
    Greensleeves, etc.

III

My men were clothed all in green,
  And they did ever wait on thee;
All this was gallant to be seen,
  And yet thou wouldst not love me.
    Greensleeves, etc.

IV

They set thee up, they took thee downe,
  They served thee with humilitie;
Thy foote might not once touch the ground,
  And yet thou wouldst not love me.
    Greensleeves, etc.

V

For everie morning when thou rose,
  I sent thee dainties orderly,
To cleare thy stomack from all woes,
  And yet thou wouldst not love me.
      Greensleeves, etc.

VI

Thou couldst desire no earthly thing,
  But still thou hadst it readily,
Thy musick still to play and sing,
  And yet thou wouldst not love me.
      Greensleeves, etc.

VII

And who did pay for all this geare
  That thou didst spend when pleased thee?
Even I that am rejected here,
  And thou disdainst to love me.
      Greensleeves, etc.

VIII

Wel, I will pray to God on hie
  That thou my constancie maist see
And that yet once before I die
  Thou wilt vouchsafe to love me.
      Greensleeves, etc.

Love's Thraldom

Those eyes that set my fan-cie on a fire!
Those crisp-ed haires which hold my hart in chaines!
Those dain-tie hands that conquered my de-sire!
That wit which of my thought doth hold the raines!
Then Love be judge, what hart may there with-stand
such eyes, such head, such wit, and such a hand?

II

Deeds of the day are fables for the night,
Sighs of desire are smokes of thoughtful teares ;
My steps are false although my path is right,
Disgrace is bold, my favour full of feares ;
Disquiet sleepe keepes audite of my Life,
Where rare content doth make displeasure rife.

III

The dolefull clocke which is the voice of time
Calles on my end before my hap is seen ;
Thus falles my hopes whose harmes have power to
    clime,

Not come to have what long in wish hath been:
I trust your love, and feare not others' hate,
Be you with me and I have Caesar's fate!

Tobacco is an Indian Weed

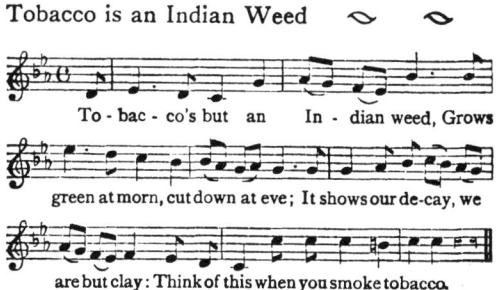

To-bac-co's but an In-dian weed, Grows green at morn, cut down at eve; It shows our de-cay, we are but clay: Think of this when you smoke tobacco.

II

The pipe, that is so lily white,
Wherein so many take delight,
Is broke with a touch—man's life is such:
Think of this when you smoke tobacco.

III

The pipe that is so foul within,
Shews how man's soul is stained with sin,
And then the fire it doth require:
Think of this when you smoke tobacco.

IV

The ashes that are left behind
Do serve to put us all in mind
That unto dust return we must :
Think of this when you smoke tobacco.

V

The smoke, that does so high ascend,
Shews us man's life must have an end,
The vapour's gone—man's life is done :
Think of this when you smoke tobacco.

EVENING

Vespers ᔕ   ᔕ   ᔕ   ᔕ   ᔕ

O BLACKBIRD, what a boy you are !
   How you do go it !
Blowing your bugle to that one sweet star—
How you do blow it !
And does she hear you, blackbird boy, so far ?
Or is it wasted breath ?
"Good Lord ! she is so bright
To-night !"
The blackbird saith.

T. E. Brown.

Bagley Wood ᔕ   ᔕ   ᔕ   ᔕ

THE night is full of stars, full of magnificence:
   Nightingales hold the wood, and fragrance
      loads the dark.
Behold, what fires august, what lights eternal !
   Hark,
What passionate music poured in passionate love's
   defence !
Breathe but the wafting wind's nocturnal frankin-
   cense !
Only to fee' this night's great heart, only to mark
The splendours and the glooms, brings back the
   patriarch
Who on Chaldean wastes found God through
   reverence.

Could we but live at will upon this perfect height,
Could we but always keep the passion of this peace,
Could we but face unshamed the look of this pure light,
Could we but win earth's heart, and give desire release:
Then were we all divine, and then were ours by right
These stars, these nightingales, these scents: then shame would cease.

Lionel Johnson.

With how sad steps, O Moon

WITH how sad steps, O Moon, thou climb'st the skies,
How silently, and with how wan a face!
What! may it be, that even in heavenly place
That busy archer his sharp arrow tries?
Sure if that long with love acquainted eyes
Can judge of love, thou feel'st a lover's case;
I read it in thy looks; thy languish'd grace
To me, that feel the like, thy state descries.
Then even of fellowship, O Moon, tell me
Is constant love deem'd there but want of wit?
Are beauties there as proud as here they be?
Do they above love to be loved, and yet
Those lovers scorn whom that love doth possess?
Do they call virtue there, ungratefulness?

Sir Philip Sidney.

Song

After the French of Rostand

OH, many a lover sighs
    Beneath the Summer skies
For black or hazel eyes
    All day;
No light of hope can mar
My whiter brighter star;
I love a Princess far
    Away.

Now you that haste to meet
Your love's returning feet
Must plead for every sweet
    Caress;
But, day and night and day,
Without a prayer to pray,
I love my far away
    Princess.

Alfred Noyes.

Autumn

AUTUMN grows old: he, like some simple one,
    In Summer's castaways is strangely clad;
    Such withered things the Winds in frolic mad
Shake from his feeble hand and forehead wan.

Autumn is sighing for his early gold,
    And in his tremble dropping his remains;
    The brook talks more, as one bereft of brains,
Who singeth loud, delirious with the cold.

O now with drowsy June one hour to be!
    Scarce waking strength to hear the hum of bees,
    Or cattle lowing under shady trees,
Knee-deep in waters loitering to the sea.

I would that drowsy June awhile were here,
    The amorous South wind carrying all the vale—
    Save that white lily true to star as pale,
Whose secret day-dream Phœbus burns to bear.

William H. Davies.

To the Moon

ART thou pale for weariness
    Of climbing heaven and gazing on the earth,
Wandering companionless
Among the stars that have a different birth,—
And ever changing, like a joyless eye
That finds no object worth its constancy?

Percy Bysshe Shelley.

A Summer's Eve

DOWN the sultry arc of day
    The burning wheels have urged their way,
And eve along the western skies,
Spreads her intermingling dyes.
Down the deep, the miry lane,
Creeking comes the empty wain,
And driver on the shaft-horse sits,
Whistling now and then by fits;
And oft with his accustom'd call,
Urging on his sluggish Ball.
The barn is still, the master's gone,
And thresher puts his jacket on,
While Dick, upon the ladder tall,
Nails the dead kite to the wall.
Here comes shepherd Jack at last,
He has penn'd the sheep-cote fast,
For 'twas but two nights before,
A lamb was eaten on the moor:
His empty wallet *Rover* carries,
Now for Jack, when near home, tarries.
With lolling tongue he runs to try,
If the horse-trough be not dry.
The milk is settled in the pans,
And supper messes in the cans;
In the hovel-carts are wheel'd,
And both the colts are drove a-field;
The horses are all bedded up,
And the ewe is with the tup,
The snare of Mister Fox is set,

The leaven laid, the thatching wet,
And Bess has slink'd away to talk
With Roger in the holly-walk.

Now, on the settle all, but Bess,
Are set to eat their supper mess;
And little Tom and roguish Kate
Are swinging on the meadow gate
Now they chat of various things,
Of taxes, ministers, and kings,
Or else tell all the village news,
How madam did the squire refuse;
How parson on his tithes was bent,
And landlord oft distrained for rent.
Thus do they talk, till in the sky
The pale-eyed moon is mounted high,
And from the alehouse drunken Ned
Has reel'd—then hasten all to bed.
The mistress sees that lazy Kate
The happing coal on kitchen grate
Has laid—while master goes throughout,
Sees shutters fast, the mastiff out,
The candles safe, the hearths all clear,
And nought from thieves or fire to fear;
Then both to bed together creep,
And join the general troop of sleep.

Henry Kirke White.

Lullaby ⌢ ⌢ ⌢ ⌢

SING lullaby, as women doe,
   Wherewith they bring their babes to rest;
And lullaby can I sing too,
   As womanly as can the best.
With lullaby they still the childe,
And if I be not much beguil'd,
Full many wanton babes have I,
Which must be still'd with lullaby.

First lullaby, my youthful yeares!
   It is nowe time to go to bed,
For crooked age and hoary hairs
   Have won the haven within my head:
With lullaby, then, youth, be still,
With lullaby content thy will;
Since courage quayles, and comes behind,
Go sleepe, and so beguile thy minde.

Next lullaby, my gazing eyes,
   Which wonted were to glance apace;
For every glasse may now suffice
   To shewe the furrowes in my face.
With lullaby, then, winke awhile,
With lullaby your lookes beguile:
Let no faire face, nor beautie brighte
Entice you eft with vaine delighte.

And lullaby, my wanton will!
   Let reason's rule nowe reigne thy thought,
Since all too late I finde by skill
   Howe deare I have thy fancies bought:

With lullaby, nowe, take thine ease,
With lullaby thy doubtes appease;
For, trust to this, if thou be still,
My body shall obey thy will.
George Gascoigne.

Tranquillity

FEAR no more the heat o' the sun
   Nor the furious winter's rages;
Thou thy worldly task hast done,
   Home art gone and ta'en thy wages:
Golden lads and girls all must,
As chimney-sweepers, come to dust.

Fear no more the frown o' the great,
   Thou art past the tyrant's stroke;
Care no more to clothe and eat;
   To thee the reed is as the oak:
The sceptre, learning, physic, must
All follow this, and come to dust.

Fear no more the lightning flash
   Nor the all-dreaded thunder-stone;
Fear not slander, censure rash;
   Thou hast finish'd joy and moan:
All lovers young, all lovers must
Consign to thee, and come to dust.

William Shakespeare

To Night

SWIFTLY walk o'er the western wave,
    Spirit of Night!
Out of the misty eastern cave,
Where, all the long and lone daylight,
Thou wovest dreams of joy and fear,
Which make thee terrible and dear,—
    Swift be thy flight!

Wrap thy form in a mantle gray,
    Star inwrought!
Blind with thine hair the eyes of Day;
Kiss her until she be wearied out,
Then wander o'er city, and sea, and land,
Touching all with thine opiate wand—
    Come, long-sought!

When I arose and saw the dawn,
    I sighed for thee;
When light rode high, and the dew was gone,
And noon lay heavy on flower and tree,
And the weary Day turned to his rest,
Lingering like an unloved guest,
    I sighed for thee.

Thy brother Death came, and cried,
    Wouldst thou me?
Thy sweet child Sleep, the filmy-eyed,
Murmured like a noontide bee,
Shall I nestle near thy side?
Wouldst thou me?—And I replied,
    No, not thee!

Death will come when thou art dead,
      Soon, too soon—
Sleep will come when thou art fled;
Of neither would I ask the boon
I ask of thee, belovèd Night—
Swift be thine approaching flight,
      Come soon, soon!

Percy Bysshe Shelley.

Kubla Khan

IN Xanadu did Kubla Khan
  A stately pleasure-dome decree:
Where Alph, the sacred river, ran
Through caverns measureless to man
    Down to a sunless sea.
So twice five miles of fertile ground
With walls and towers were girdled round:
And here were gardens bright with sinuous rills,
Where blossomed many an incense-bearing tree;
And here were forests ancient as the hills,
Enfolding sunny spots of greenery.
But oh! that deep romantic chasm which slanted
Down the green hill athwart a cedarn cover!
A savage place! as holy and enchanted
As e'er beneath a waning moon was haunted
By woman wailing for her demon-lover!
And from this chasm, with ceaseless turmoil seething,
As if this earth in fast thick pants were breathing,
A mighty fountain momently was forced:
Amid whose swift half-intermitted burst

Huge fragments vaulted like rebounding hail,
Or chaffy grain beneath the thresher's flail :
And 'mid these dancing rocks at once and ever
It flung up momently the sacred river.

Five miles meandering with a mazy motion
Through wood and dale the sacred river ran,
Then reached the caverns measureless to man,
And sank in tumult to a lifeless ocean :
And 'mid this tumult Kubla heard from far
Ancestral voices prophesying war !

    The shadow of the dome of pleasure
    Floated midway on the waves ;
    Where was heard the mingled measure
    From the fountains and the caves.
It was a miracle of rare device,
A sunny pleasure-dome with caves of ice !

    A damsel with a dulcimer
    In a vision once I saw :
    It was an Abyssinian maid,
    And on her dulcimer she played.
    Singing of Mount Abora.
    Could I revive within me
    Her symphony and song,
    To such a deep delight 'twould win me,
That with music loud and long,
I would build that dome in air,
That sunny dome ! those caves of ice !

And all who heard should see them there,
And all should cry, Beware ! Beware !
His flashing eyes, his floating hair !
Weave a circle round him thrice,
And close your eyes with holy dread,
For he on honey-dew hath fed,
And drunk the milk of Paradise.

Samuel Taylor Coleridge.

To Autumn

SEASON of mists and mellow fruitfulness !
  Close bosom-friend of the maturing sun ;
Conspiring with him how to load and bless
  With fruit the vines that round the thatch-eaves run ;
To bend with apples the moss'd cottage trees,
  And fill all fruit with ripeness to the core ;
    To swell the gourd, and plump the hazel shells
  With a sweet kernel ; to set budding more,
And still more, later flowers for the bees,
Until they think warm day will never cease,
    For Summer has o'er-brimm'd their clammy cells.

Who hath not seen thee oft amid thy store ?
  Sometimes whoever seeks abroad may find
Thee sitting careless on a granary floor,
  Thy hair soft-lifted by the winnowing wind ;

Or on a half-reap'd furrow sound asleep,
   Drowsed with the fume of poppies, while thy hook
     Spares the next swath and all its twined flowers.
And sometimes like a gleaner thou dost keep
   Steady thy laden head across a brook ;
   Or by a cider-press, with patient look,
     Thou watchest the last oozings, hour by hour.

Where are the songs of Spring? Ay, where are they?
   Think not of them, thou hast thy music too,
     While barred clouds bloom the soft-dying day,
And touch the stubble-plains with rosy hue ;
   Then in a wailful choir, the small gnats mourn
   Among the river sallows, borne aloft
     Or sinking as the light wind lives or dies ;
And full-grown lambs loud bleat from hilly bourn ;
   Hedge-crickets sing ; and now with treble soft
   The redbreast whistles from a garden-croft,
     And gathering swallows twitter in the skies.

                    John Keats.

Autumn

O AUTUMN, laden with fruit, and stained
   With the blood of the grape, pass not, but sit
Beneath my shady roof; there thou mayst rest,
And tune thy jolly voice to my fresh pipe,
And all the daughters of the year shall dance !
Sing now the lusty songs of fruits and flowers.

"The narrow bud opens her beauties to
The sun, and love runs in her thrilling veins;
Blossoms hang round the brows of Morning, and
Flourish down the bright cheek of modest Eve,
Till clustering Summer breaks forth into singing,
And feathered clouds strew flowers round her head.

"The Spirits of the Air live on the smells
Of fruit; and Joy, with pinions light, roves round
The gardens, or sits singing in the trees."
Thus sang the jolly Autumn as he sat;
Then rose, girded himself, and o'er the bleak
Hills fled from our sight; but left his golden load.

William Blake.

Ave Maria!

AVE MARIA! blessed be the hour!
   The time, the clime, the spot, where I so oft
Have felt that moment in its fullest power
   Sink o'er the earth so beautiful and soft,
While swung the deep bell in the distant tower,
   Or the faint dying day-hymn stole aloft,
And not a breath crept through the rosy air,
And yet the forest leaves seem'd stirr'd with prayer.

Ave Maria! 'tis the hour of prayer!
   Ave Maria! 'tis the hour of love!
Ave Maria! may our spirits dare
   Look up to thine and to thy Son's above!

Ave Maria! oh that face so fair!
  Those downcast eyes beneath the Almighty
    dove—
What though 'tis but a pictured image?—strike—
That painting is no idol,—'tis too like.

Some kinder casuists are pleased to say,
  In nameless print—that I have no devotion;
But set those persons down with me to pray,
  And you will see who has the properest notion
Of getting into heaven the shortest way;
  My altars are the mountains and the ocean,
Earth, air, stars,—all that springs from the great
    Whole,
Who hath produced, and will receive the soul.

Sweet hour of twilight!—in the solitude
  Of the pine forest, and the silent shore
Which bounds Ravenna's immemorial wood,
  Rooted where once the Adrian wave flow'd o'er,
To where the last Cæsarean fortress stood,
  Evergreen forest! which Boccaccio's lore
And Dryden's lay made haunted ground to me,
How have I loved the twilight hour and thee!

The shrill cicalas, people of the pine,
  Making their summer lives one ceaseless song,
Were the sole echoes, save my steed's and mine,
  And vesper's bell that rose the boughs along;
The spectre huntsman of Onesti's line,
  His hell-dogs, and their chase, and the fair throng
Which learn'd from this example not to fly
From a true lover,—shadow'd my mind's eye.

Oh, Hesperus! thou bringest all good things—
  Home to the weary, to the hungry cheer,
To the young bird the parent's brooding wings,
  The welcome stall to the o'erlabour'd steer;
Whate'er of peace about our hearthstone clings,
  Whate'er our household gods protect of dear,
Are gather'd round us by thy look of rest;
Thou bring'st the child, too, to the mother's breast

Soft hour! which wakes the wish and melts the heart
  Of those who sail the seas, on the first day
When they from their sweet friends are torn apart;
  Or fills with love the pilgrim on his way
As the far bell of vesper makes him start,
  Seeming to weep the dying day's decay;
Is this a fancy which our reason scorns?
Ah! surely nothing dies but something mourns!

When Nero perish'd by the justest doom
  Which ever the destroyer yet destroyed,
Amidst the roar of liberated Rome,
  Of nations freed, and the world overjoy'd,
Some hands unseen strew'd flowers upon his tomb:
  Perhaps the weakness of a heart not void
Of feeling for some kindness done, when power
Had left the wretch an uncorrupted hour.

Lord Byron.

Milking Time

COME, pretty Phyllis, you are late!
   The cows are crowding round the gate.
An hour, or more, the sun has set;
The stars are out; the grass is wet;
The glow-worms shine; the beetles hum;
The moon is near—come, Phyllis, come!

The black cow thrusts her brass-tipped horns
Among the quick and bramble-thorns;
The red cow jerks the padlock chain;
The dun cow shakes her bell again,
And round and round the chestnut tree
The white cow bellows lustily.

The wistful nightingales complain
From bush to bush along the lane;
The ringdoves coo from fir to fir
And cannot sleep because of her;
The evejars prate on every side—
O, Phyllis, where do you abide?

Now faeries, fays, elves, goblins, go
And find out where she lingers so,
And pinch her nose and chin and ears,
Nor heed her cries, nor heed her tears:
At any farm 'twould be a crime
To be so late at milking time.

Charles Dalmon.

Romance

WILD spirit of the charmèd quest
    For what the heart within us craves!
O haunter of the purple caves
Beyond the sunset in the West!
—Spaces of glamour and unrest
Aërial, perilous, possessed
Of all the music of the waves—
When down those occidental halls
Deathward the sun in thunder gropes
O'er multitudes of sounding slopes
And leagues of burnished waterfalls,
And seas of gold that break and break
In music on the shores, and wake
Far echoes of the mountain walls
Where all the faery forests shake—
He finds thee, wistful, with thy lyre,
Thy face grown holy with desire,
Beside the deep that calls and calls;
And round about thee where thou art
He spills the vials of his heart
In glory and in flakes of fire.

Gerald Gould.

The Poet in the Clouds

O! it is pleasant, with a heart at ease,
    Just after sunset, or by moonlight skies,
To make the shifting clouds be what you please,
    Or let the easily persuaded eyes

Own each quaint likeness issuing from the mould
  Of a friend's fancy ; or with head bent low
And cheek aslant see rivers flow with gold
  'Twixt crimson banks ; and then, a traveller, go
From mount to mount through Cloudland, gorgeous land !
  Or listening to the tide, with closed sight,
Be that blind bard, who on the Chian strand
  By those deep sounds possessed with inward light,
Beheld the Iliad and the Odyssee
  Rise to the swelling of the voiceful sea.

Samuel Taylor Coleridge.

The Unexplored ○   ○   ○   ○

OUT of lonely seas we sailed
    After dusk, and crossed the bar
Ere the darkness wholly veiled
    Haven shores and lands afar ;
Ere the path of wild-rose light
O'er the hills had faded quite,
Or the shore-light's golden rays
Glowed across the water-ways.

Wonderlands of which we dreamed
    Over the unventured seas
Never more enchanted seemed,
    Never lovelier than these—

These that, hidden till the dawn
  Now no boundary confines,
Save where starry skies have drawn
  Silvery horizon lines.

There, between the veiled and shown,
Wonders hidden are our own;
Forest voices whisper there
Lore of days that never were;
Secrets vision hides we find
Written in the undefined;
Revelations in the guessed,
Treasures in the unpossessed.

Darker over waters dark,
  Loom the shores; and still remains,
Here and there, a light to mark
  Ships along the haven lanes,
Softer, over ripples soft,
  Far away the sea-winds blow;
Fairer than the stars aloft
  Shine the stars in depths below.

Ah! what seek we? Even now
While we wonder, we endow
All things near us and afar
With the dreams that nowhere are:
Reading into the unknown
Hopes that we have long outgrown,
Weaving into the unseen
Tidings of the might-have-been.

Soon along the eastern rim
  Light shall steal, and silver mist
Flash to rose, and uplands dim
  Wake in folds of amethyst.
Soon shall tidings twilight told,
  Soon shall pathways starlight drew
Vanish in the morning's gold,
  Hide behind the noonday's blue.

Now, till morn, remain our own
  Magic shores of old surmise,
Peaks no morning can dethrone,
  Lands that know no boundaries.
There the unfulfilled abides ;
  There the touch of night unbars
Gates of ways that noonday hides,
  Paths that reach beyond the stars.

Sidney Royse Lysaght.

The Darkling Thrush

I LEANT upon a coppice gate
  When Frost was spectre-gray,
And Winter's dregs made desolate
  The weakening eye of day.
The tangled bine-stems scored the sky
  Like strings from broken lyres,
And all mankind that haunted nigh
  Had sought their household fires.

The land's sharp features seemed to be
   The Century's corpse outleant,
His crypt the cloudy canopy,
   The wind his death-lament.
The ancient pulse of germ and birth
   Was shrunken hard and dry,
And every spirit upon earth
   Seemed fervourless as I.

At once a voice outburst among
   The bleak twigs overhead,
In a full-hearted evensong
   Of joy illimited ;
An aged thrush, frail, gaunt, and small,
   In blast-beruffled plume,
Had chosen thus to fling his soul
   Upon the growing gloom.

So little cause for carollings
   Of such ecstatic sound
Was written on terrestrial things
   Afar or nigh around,
That I could think there trembled through
   His happy good-night air
Some blessed Hope, whereof he knew
   And I was unaware.

Thomas Hardy

Vertue ～ ～ ～ ～ ～

SWEET day, so cool, so calm, so bright,
　The bridall of the earth and skie:
The dew shall weep thy fall to night;
　　　For thou must die.

Sweet rose, whose hue angrie and brave
Bids the rash gazer wipe his eye:
Thy root is ever in its grave,
　　　And thou must die.

Sweet spring, full of sweet dayes and roses,
A box where sweets compacted lie;
My musick shows ye have your closes,
　　　And all must die.

Onely a sweet and vertuous soul,
Like season'd timber, never gives;
But though the whole world turns to coal,
　　　Then chiefly lives.
　　　　　　　　　　George Herbert.

This only Grant Me ～ ～ ～

THIS only grant me, that my means may lye
　Too low for Envy, for Contempt too high.
　Some Honour I would have
Not from great deeds, but good alone.
Th' unknown are better than ill known.
　Rumour can ope the Grave.
Acquaintance I would have, but when't depends
Not on the number, but the choice of Friends.

Books should, not business, entertain the Light,
And sleep, as undisturb'd as Death, the Night;
   My House a Cottage, more
Than Palace, and should fitting be
For all my Use, no Luxurie;
   My Garden painted o'er
With Nature's hand, not Art's; and pleasures yield,
Horace might envy in his Sabine field.

Thus would I double my Life's fading space,
For he that runs it well, twice runs his race.
   And in this true delight,
These unbought sports, that happy State,
I would not fear nor wish my fate,
   But boldly say each night,
To-morrow let my Sun his beams display,
Or in clouds hide them; I have liv'd to-day.
                      Abraham Cowley.

The Message of the March Wind

FAIR now is the springtide, now earth lies beholding
With the eyes of a lover, the face of the sun;
Long lasteth the daylight, and hope is enfolding
The green-growing acres with increase begun.

Now sweet, sweet it is through the land to be straying
'Mid the birds and the blossoms and the beasts of
   the field;
Love mingles with love, and no evil is weighing
On thy heart or mine, where all sorrow is healed

From township to township, o'er down and by
    tillage
Fair, far have we wandered and long was the day ;
But now cometh eve at the end of the village,
Where over the grey wall the church riseth grey.

There is wind in the twilight ; in the white road
    before us
The straw from the ox-yard is blowing about ;
The moon's rim is rising, a star glitters o'er us,
And the vane on the spire-top is swinging in doubt.

Down there dips the highway, toward the bridge
    crossing over
The brook that runs on to the Thames and the sea.
Draw closer, my sweet, we are lover and lover ;
This eve art thou given to gladness and me.

Shall we be glad always? Come closer and hearken:
Three fields further on, as they told me down there,
When the young moon has set, if the March sky
    should darken,
We might see from the hill-top the great city's glare.

Hark, the wind in the elm-boughs ! From London
    it bloweth,
And telleth of gold, and of hope and unrest ;
Of power that helps not; of wisdom that knoweth,
But teacheth not aught of the worst and the best.

Of the rich men it telleth, and strange is the story
How they have, and they hanker, and grip far and
  wide;
And they live and they die, and the earth and its
  glory
Have been but a burden they scarce might abide.

Hark! the March wind again of a people is telling;
Of the life that they live there, so haggard and
  grim,
That if we and our love amidst them had been
  dwelling
My fondness had faltered, thy beauty grown dim.

This land we have loved in our love and our leisure
For them hangs in heaven, high out of their reach;
The wide hills o'er the sea plain for them have no
  pleasure,
The grey homes of their fathers no story to teach.

The singers have sung and the builders have builded,
The painters have fashioned their tales of delight;
For what and for whom hath the world's book been
  gilded,
When all is for these but the blackness of night?

How long, and for what is their patience abiding?
How oft and how oft shall their story be told,
While the hope that none seeketh in darkness is
  hiding
And in grief and in sorrow the world groweth old?

• • • • •

Come back to the inn, love, and the lights and the
    fire,
And the fiddler's old tune and the shuffling of feet;
For there in a while shall be rest and desire,
And there shall the morrow's uprising be sweet.

Yet, love, as we wend, the wind bloweth behind us,
And beareth the last tale it telleth to-night,
How here in the springtide the message shall find
    us;
For the hope that none seeketh is coming to light.

Like the seed of mid-winter, unheeded, unperished,
Like the autumn-sown wheat 'neath the snow lying
    green,
Like the love that o'ertook us, unawares and un-
    cherished,
Like the babe 'neath thy girdle that groweth un-
    seen;

So the hope of the people now buddeth and groweth,
Rest fadeth before it, and blindness and fear;
It biddeth us learn all the wisdom it knoweth;
It hath found us and held us, and biddeth us hear:

For it beareth the message: "Rise up on the morrow
And go on your ways toward the doubt and the
    strife;
Join hope to our hope and blend sorrow with sorrow,
And seek for men's love in the short days of life."

But lo, the old inn, and the lights, and the fire,
And the fiddler's old tune and the shuffling of feet;
Soon for us shall be quiet and rest and desire
And to-morrow's uprising to deeds shall be sweet.

William Morris.

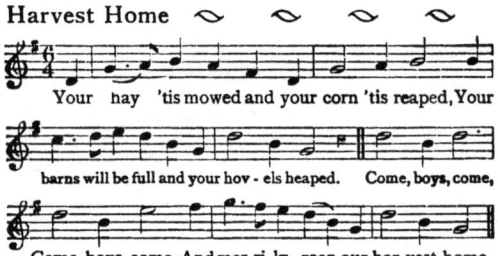

Your hay 'tis mowed and your corn 'tis reaped, Your barns will be full and your hov-els heaped. Come, boys, come, Come, boys, come, And mer-ri-ly roar our har-vest-home.

II

We ha' cheated the Parson, we'll cheat him agen,
For why should a Blockhead ha' one in ten?
　　　One in ten,
　　　One in ten,
For why should a Blockhead ha' one in ten?

III

For prating too long like a Book-learnt Sot,
Till Pudding and Dumpling are burnt to Pot;
　　　Burnt to Pot, etc.

IV

We'll toss off our Ale till we cannot stand,
And Hey for the Honour of old England;
　　　Old England, etc.

Harvest home,
Harvest home,
And merrily roar our Harvest home.

Spanish Ladies

From Cecil Sharp

Farewell and a-dieu to you, Spanish la-dies, Fare-well and a-dieu to you, la-dies of Spain; For we've re-ceived or-ders to sail for old England, But we hope that we one day may see you a-gain.

From John Masefield

Farewell and a-dieu to you, Spanish la-dies, Fare-well and a-dieu to you, la-dies of Spain; For we've re-ceived or-ders to sail for old England, But we hope that we one day may see you a-gain.

II

We hove our ship to when the wind was sou'-west, boys,
We hove our ship to for to strike soundings clear,
Then we filled our main tops'l and bore right away, boys,
And right up the Channel of England did steer.

III

The first land we made it was known as the Deadman,
Next Ramshead near Plymouth, Start, Portland and Wight,
We sailèd past Beachy, past Fairley and Dungeness,
And then bore away for the South Foreland Light.

IV

Then the sign it was made for the grand fleet to anchor,
All in the Downs that night for to meet,
Then it's stand by your stoppers, let go your shank-painters,
Haul all your clew-garnets, stick out tacks and sheets.

V

So let every man toss off his full bumper,
Let every man toss off his full bowl,
We'll drink and be jolly, and drown melancholy,
With a health to each jovial and true-hearted soul.

Chorus.

We'll rant and we'll roar like true British sailors,
We'll range and we'll roam over all the salt seas,
Until we strike soundings in the Channel of
    England:
From Ushant to Scilly 'tis thirty-five leagues.

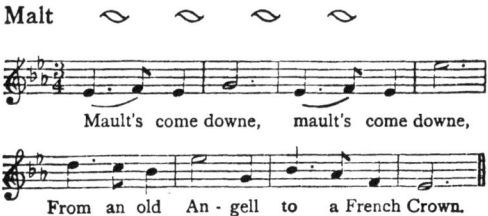

II

There's never a maide in all this Towne,
But well she knowes that Mault's come downe.
    Mault's come downe, etc.

III

The greatest Drunkards in this Towne
Are very glad that Mault's come downe.
    Mault's come downe, etc.

When the King enjoys His Own again

What book-er can prog-nos-ti-cate Con-cern-ing kings or king-doms' fate? I think my-self to be as wise As he that gaz-eth on the skies; My skill goes be-yond the depths of a pond or riv-ers in the great-est rain, Where-by I can tell all things will be well When the king en-joys his own a-gain.

II

There's neither Swallow, Dove nor Dade,
Can soar more high or deeper wade;
Nor show a reason from the stars
What causeth peace or civil wars;
The man in the moon may wear out his shon
By running after Charles his wain;
But all's to no end, for the times will not mend
Till the King enjoy his own again.

III

Though for a time we see Whitehall
With cobwebs hanging on the wall,
Instead of silk and silver brave
Which formerly it used to have,
With rich perfume in every room,
Delightful in that princely train
Which again you shall see when the time it shall be
That the King enjoys his own again.

IV

Full forty years the royal crown
Hath been his father's and his own,
And is there any one but he
That in the same should sharer be?
For who better may the sceptre sway
Than he that hath such right to reign?
Then let's hope for a peace, for the wars will not cease
Till the King enjoys his own again.

V

Till then upon Ararat's hill
My hope shall cast her anchor still,
Until I see some peaceful dove
Bring home the branch I dearly love.
Then will I wait till the waters abate,
Which now disturb my troubled brain,
Else never rejoice till I hear the voice
That the King enjoys his own again.

Martin Parker.

When Thou must Home

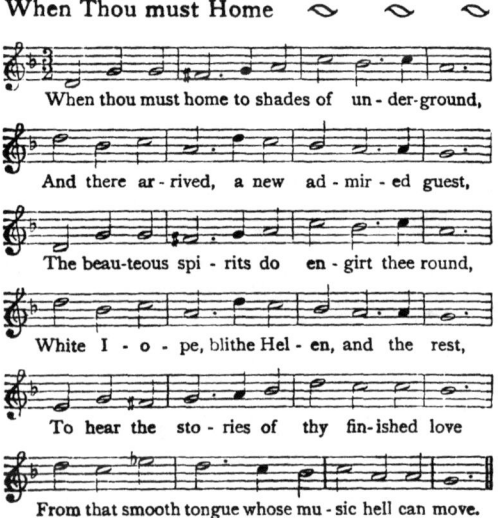

When thou must home to shades of un-der-ground,
And there ar-rived, a new ad-mir-ed guest,
The beau-teous spi-rits do en-girt thee round,
White I-o-pe, blithe Hel-en, and the rest,
To hear the sto-ries of thy fin-ished love
From that smooth tongue whose mu-sic hell can move.

II

Then wilt thou speak of banqueting delights,
Of masques and revels which sweet Youth did make,
Of tourneys and great challenges of knights,
And all these triumphs for thy beauty's sake :
When thou hast told these honours done to thee,
Then tell, O tell, how thou didst murder me !

Thomas Campion.

Three Men of Gotham

Air: "Courtiers"

Sea-men three, what men be ye?......
Gotham's three wise men be we. Whither in your
boat so free? To rake the moon from out the sea. The
bowl goes trim, the moon doth shine, And our ballast
is old wine And your ballast is old wine.

II

Who art thou, so fast adrift?
I am he they call Old Care.
Here on board we will thee lift.
No: I may not enter there.
Wherefore so? 'Tis Jove's decree,
In a bowl Care may not be.—
In a bowl Care may not be.

III

Fear ye not the waves that roll?
No: in charmèd bowl we swim.
What the charm that floats the bowl?

Water may not pass the brim,
The bowl goes trim. The moon doth shine,
And our ballast is old wine.—
And your ballast is old wine.

Thomas Love Peacock.

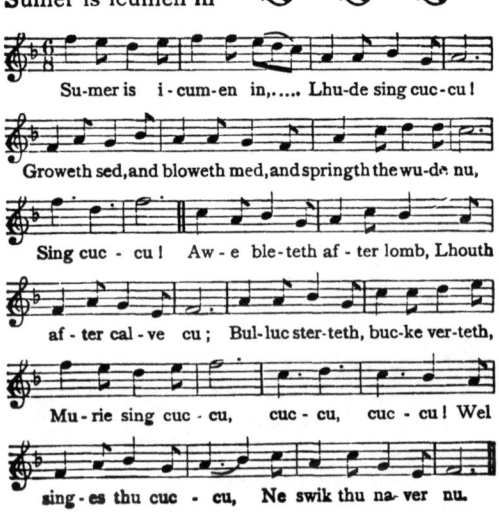

Made in the USA
Middletown, DE
26 September 2017